Praise for *Protect Your People*

"The stories in *Protect Your People* provide a window into what is possible when people come together to face the violence of legal systems with community, compassion, and strength. It is a must-read for its inspiring collective account of how we can take down mass incarceration—but only if we do it together, taking our cues from those who are closest to the problem."
—Jocelyn Simonson, author of *Radical Acts of Justice: How Ordinary People Are Dismantling Incarceration* and professor of law and associate dean for research and scholarship, Brooklyn Law School

"The model of participatory defense pioneered by Silicon Valley De-Bug is one of the most important and inspiring developments of the last two decades in the fight against mass incarceration. You won't be the same after reading this book, and you'll think differently about how you can get involved in your community."
—Alec Karakatsanis, author of *Usual Cruelty: The Complicity of Lawyers in the Criminal Injustice System* and founder of the Civil Rights Corps

"The pretrial process is often opaque—if not incomprehensible. *Protect Your People* busts through these walls by not only explaining how the carceral system works, but more importantly, how families and communities can come together and wrench their loved ones from its jaws."
—Victoria Law, journalist and co-author of *Prison by Any Other Name: The Harmful Consequences of Popular Reforms*

"Having spent a career building a movement of public defenders to help transform the criminal legal system, I am all too aware that human beings are easily processed into cages when the voices, stories, and power of justice-impacted families and communities are suppressed. Through participatory defense these voices are heard, stories are told, and power is realized. It is a model that strengthens our work as justice advocates by breaking down walls between the court system and the people it impacts most directly. The lessons in this book will make all of us who care about justice more effective."

—Jonathan Rapping, the author of *Gideon's Promise: A Public Defender Movement to Transform Criminal Justice*

"Participatory Defense gives marginalized communities access to justice commonly denied to them. It gave my friend the support she needed to show that her son suffered from mental health illness as opposed to being seen just as a criminal justice problem. It gave my other dear friend access to freedom after serving a couple decades and a daughter a chance to welcome her father home. It gave my son a road map to engage in the fight to free his son, and the hope we all need as a family."

—Dorsey Nunn, executive director of Legal Services for Prisoners with Children

"How do we free people caught in the criminal legal system? As we work to dismantle this prison industrial complex we need multiple ways to organize for the freedom of those currently incarcerated! Jayadev's moving, detailed, and timely collection offers a range of ideas, examples, and reflections from people who are working collaboratively to free people while also keeping our eyes on the prize."

—Erica R. Meiners, co-author of both *Abolition. Feminism. Now.* and *The Feminist and the Sex Offender: Confronting Sexual Harm, Ending State Violence*

Raj Jayadev is the co-founder of Silicon Valley De-Bug, a community organizing, advocacy, and multimedia storytelling organization. His work has been featured in the *New York Times*, *Time*, the *San Francisco Chronicle*, *HuffPost*, on PBS, the BBC, and other media outlets across the country. He is a 2018 MacArthur "genius" fellow and lives in San Jose, California, with his wife and son.

PROTECT YOUR PEOPLE

How Ordinary Families Are Using
Participatory Defense to Challenge
Mass Incarceration

RAJ JAYADEV

NEW YORK
LONDON

© 2024 by Raj Jayadev, William Bentley, Robert Blair, Blanca Bosquez, Charisse Domingo, DeVonté Douglass, Sarait Escorza, Natalie Gonzalez, Dr. Dorothy Johnson-Speight, Dawn Harrington, Andréa Hudson, Gicola Lane, Heather Lewis, Gail Noble, Fox Richardson, Robert Richardson, Imani Mfalme Shu'la, Andre Simms, Phal Sok, John Vasquez, Ramon Vasquez, Marcel Woodruff

Published in the United States by The New Press, New York, 2024
Distributed by Two Rivers Distribution

ISBN 978-1-62097-700-2 (pb)
ISBN 978-1-62097-806-1 (ebook)
CIP data is available

The New Press publishes books that promote and enrich public discussion and understanding of the issues vital to our democracy and to a more equitable world. These books are made possible by the enthusiasm of our readers; the support of a committed group of donors, large and small; the collaboration of our many partners in the independent media and the not-for-profit sector; booksellers, who often hand-sell New Press books; librarians; and above all by our authors.

www.thenewpress.com

Composition by Dix Digital Prepress and Design
This book was set in Garamond Premier Pro

Printed in the United States of America

10 9 8 7 6 5 4 3 2 1

CONTENTS

PROTECT YOUR PEOPLE

INTRODUCTION

THE STORY OF PARTICIPATORY DEFENSE

The line waiting to get into the courthouse has to be one of the most stress-filled and anxious gatherings of people in any city, on any given day. In my home of San Jose, California, the afternoon line often runs a block long, snaking around the corner and bleeding into the sidewalk. The line is mainly made up of Black and Brown folks of all ages—some who are there to attend to their own cases, others showing up to support a loved one who has a court hearing. There are moms holding little kids' hands, people in various uniforms who took off work to attend court, elders trying to decipher folded up court paperwork, folks running from the nearby light rail station, worried they will be late. Different native tongues can be heard, and people's eyes are constantly scanning the area for friends, family, and attorneys—essential support.

As unique as each of the stories are, the common questions that weigh on everyone create an unspoken comradery. What will happen once they walk through the court doors? Will the person they are there for be able to walk out with them or will they be kept in jail? Will what happens at today's court hearing forever change the rest of their life, their family's lives?

There are over 2.5 million people incarcerated in the United

States, including over 500,000 people being held in jails who have not even been convicted of a crime. Another 4.5 million are on probation or parole. These figures mean the United States is the largest jailer in the world by far. Incarceration not only devastates those it locks away, it also impacts their families and loved ones. Currently one in four American adults has had a sibling incarcerated. One in five has had a parent sent to jail or prison. One in eight has had a child incarcerated.

While prisons, jails, and detention centers are the structures where people are held captive by mass incarceration, the courts are where the terms are first decided. And every day, people are processed through the courts to prisons and jails at blinding speed and striking scale. The courthouse is the origin story of every person held, and every person harmed, through mass incarceration in America. It is the engine of incarceration, where police arrests become charges, where charges become convictions, and where convictions become sentences. And to feed the numbers of mass incarceration of today, the courts operate as a high-speed carceral assembly line, driven by the value of efficiency rather than justice.

But the courts are also where the assembly line of incarceration can be disrupted and challenged. It means that the courthouse can be a site of resistance, a place where those waiting in line to face or bear witness to incarceration can become the force that stands up against it. The irony of the growth of mass incarceration is that, in its wake of destruction, it is creating a movement—comprised of the incarcerated, their families and communities—that has the size, commitment, and strength to dismantle it and bring about its undoing.

Through a community-organizing model we call participatory defense, we are seeing a call taking root to fight mass incarceration at the court by families and communities, winning freedom, and building a liberatory and transformative movement with every new victory. Participatory defense is a strategic practice for families and communities to intervene in and ultimately positively impact the outcome of court cases, transforming the landscape of power in the courts. Family here goes beyond blood to include the friends, neighbors, partners, coaches, and others who care about the person about to walk through those courthouse doors. The model includes a range of approaches and tactics that, taken together, have gotten charges and sentences reduced or dropped altogether. In the process of these struggles, we have seen leaders emerge from the most difficult times in their lives and communities become stronger in the face of carceral forces that intended to shrink their power. We have seen communities across the country use participatory defense to protect their people, to reunite their families, and to free their loved ones. This book is an introduction to some of those participatory defense practitioners, the stories that defined their struggles, and what they did to win.

The De-Bug Story

Silicon Valley De-Bug is a community organization in San Jose, California. Since coming together in 2001, we have been a platform for local communities left out of the exclusionary Silicon Valley tech economy—immigrants and young people of color working minimum-wage temp jobs, the formerly incarcerated, families struggling to make rent in one of the costliest places to live in the country—to organize and to create campaigns, media, and other initiatives for racial and economic justice. Over the years, De-Bug has become a cultural, social, and political touchstone in San Jose. I've been there since the beginning, through all the changes in San Jose over the years, and despite evolving focuses and expressions of the work, De-Bug has remained a steadfast space of support for the community.

The families I work with there have built up participatory defense and used this approach to impact the cases of their loved ones since 2006. But Silicon Valley De-Bug didn't start with our efforts at the court. Instead, our organizing journey to participatory defense started where the violence of the system is first inflicted on the community—police contact.

Rudy Cardenas was killed in 2004 by a state law enforcement agent blocks away from where we operated in downtown San Jose. It was a case of mistaken identity: the police went to the home of the person who missed a meeting with his parole officer, but no one was home. As they were waiting outside, Rudy drove by. Going off of a vague description, they chased him in unmarked cars, and when Rudy got out of his car, one of the officers in pursuit, Officer Michael Walker, shot him in the back, killing him.

A number of us from De-Bug went to a vigil the family held, and upon first meeting them, became determined to support the family in their powerful journey to get justice for Rudy, whatever that meant to them. By galvanizing community support, the family secured the first open grand jury in the history of the county to indict the officer who killed Rudy. Though Michael Walker was eventually acquitted at trial, it was clear that the organizing—the rallies, marches, calls for transparency and accountability from the family and the community—had transformed what was possible, not just for Rudy's family, but for the larger community's call to end police violence.

De-Bug became the place where families who lost loved ones to police violence came together to launch their campaigns and advance powerful collective demands for policy changes in the police department and city. But it soon grew to include more than just responding to the most lethal aspects of policing. People began to come to De-Bug when they were assaulted by police, racially profiled, or harassed. Together, these folks would grow a

4

local community force that was pushing back against a wide range of abuses. Their organizing led to changes in arresting practices and use-of-force policies, and made police accountability a central political issue in a city that always tried to ignore that violence.

As more people started coming to De-Bug with their experiences of police violence, a trend emerged: they began to talk about other assaults by the system, including criminal charges, prosecutions, and incarcerations. Not only were they tased, but they were also charged with resisting arrest. Not only were they pulled over because they had been racially profiled, but it also resulted in a probation violation. The incident with the police was last week, and now they had court next week.

As organizers, we knew how to march, rally, and hold press conferences—how to flex community power against police violence. But the courts were a different thing. Without necessarily saying it out loud, we assumed we couldn't make change in the courts, because that was the arena of lawyers and judges. But what that ultimately meant was that we would let people we knew, loved, and called a part of our community face the court system alone. Without realizing it, we were relinquishing our fundamental belief in collective power at the precise moment it was most needed to protect our people.

Once they were forced to make decisions that might risk their future freedom while sitting alone in a jail cell, the overwhelming majority of the people who told us about the charges they faced in court took plea deals. In fact, over 90 percent of all cases nationally are "resolved" through a plea deal, meaning the majority of people charged with a crime never see the "day in court" fantasy featured so prominently in movies and TV shows. After taking a plea deal, they faced a common story: a long jail commitment, a lengthy prison sentence, even deportations after time in prison or jail was done. Families were torn apart and communities were decimated—permanent harm that would leave a wake of damage across generations.

After bearing witness to this, we gave up on the limiting perspective that courts were only for lawyers. Aram James, a retired public defender whom we knew through our organizing to end police killings, encouraged us. He took the cloak off the court and let us know that our movement on the streets could be just as impactful in the courtroom. Prosecutors could be held accountable just like the police could; the systemic racism that informed criminal charges and sentencing could be challenged just as we challenged the use of a gun or baton by a cop. We did this by drawing from the only science we knew: fundamental community organizing.

Community organizing is the consistent force of justice that has been effective throughout history—when a targeted, oppressed community comes together to fight back against and ultimately defeat institutions of power. Looking around us, we saw it in every aspect of our public lives: how parents and students are fixing education, how patients are transforming health care, and how every successful workers' movement has defeated powerful corporations and greedy industries across the globe. We are stronger together than alone. Why not apply the same ethic to the criminal punishment system?

The criminal court system, by design, has been insulated from this transformative community organizing dynamic. It's clear by the coded language the system uses, the law enforcement officers armed with guns at the courthouse door, and the way the judges are seated above everyone else that the criminal court system intends to isolate and individualize people facing charges. But that means that the power of community holds the potential, when moving as a collective force, to disrupt and dismantle this court system.

For us, this community started when people we knew who had cases started talking through their unique situations together. It was Blanca, whose teenage son Rudy was being accused of masterminding a robbery, despite the fact that he was severely developmentally delayed and was never outside of his family's care. It was Cecilia, whose father was picked up when he was looking for work as a day laborer and now faced a consequential deportation order in addition to criminal charges. When Lamar was pulled over and suspected he had been racially profiled by the police, he asked why he had been stopped. He was subsequently beaten and pepper sprayed by a sheriff and charged with resisting arrest. Blanca, Rudy, Cecilia, Lamar, and his mother Gail all came to De-Bug on a Sunday afternoon. The simple act of coming together was the beginning of a powerful movement.

At the De-Bug office, on a whiteboard, beneath the names of each person who had an active court case, we took an inventory of what we already knew and listed any possible actions we could take to impact the case. What are the charges? Is there a defense attorney involved? Has bail been set? Do we have the police report? When is the next court date? These questions helped identify what the action steps could be. For instance, if someone had a court date coming up that week, we would offer to show up, letting the judge and prosecutor know that the person facing charges was part of a supportive community that was invested in the person's future and well-being. Or it might be a session to review the police report and identify the falsehoods and inconsistencies. A family's action step might be collecting letters of future employment opportunities for a person to get to the defense attorney before they went their next hearing.

Blanca, Rudy, Cecilia, Lamar, and Gail and other families came back the next week, and the week after that. Each time, they shared updates, and together we figured out a new set of action steps. Each of their cases ended in the way they had hoped and worked toward: charges dropped, no jail or detention time. And to a person they each wanted to support other families who were starting the same treacherous road they once walked and were now free from. They knew what it felt like to be alone, and while they couldn't magically make a charge go away or promise every situation would end favorably, they could definitely say to those walking through our doors that they wouldn't be alone.

We never made flyers for these meetings, nor did we do any outreach or promotion. But when people who came to the Sunday meetings visited their loved ones in jail, they'd invite other families doing jail visits to the meetings. In this way, word spread organically in the community and the jail that there was a space for families to support each other's court cases.

Over time, these Sunday meetings were given a name, though it was born out of tragedy. On January 23, 2010, Albert Cobarrubias was shot and killed, becoming the first homicide of the year in San Jose. He was thirty-one years old and had been volunteering at the Sunday meetings for years. He was more disciplined than the rest of us. He was a father, had a military background, and would always show up early to set the chairs up and get the room ready and make fun of us for being late. He showed up for families in court and spread the word about the meetings to families from his part of town in East San Jose. He died on a Saturday evening. That Sunday, the families decided we would name the meetings at De-Bug after him, so he would always be with us as we fought for freedom. It would allow us to say his name when inviting people over. Sunday meetings officially became known as the Albert Cobarrubias Justice Project (ACJP).

When people attended the ACJP meeting for the first time, they often didn't know what they were walking into. Some, assuming it was a legal clinic, would ask, "Who is the attorney here?" or "Is this where I get an attorney?" Over time, we settled into the practice of providing an introductory welcome whenever newcomers would join, which clarified that we weren't providing a service; instead, we were doing community organizing: we were supporting *their* advocacy for their loved one. *They* were the agent of change. It's why we never used the word "client" to refer to whoever came to meetings, because that word that presumes someone is a recipient of a service rather than the driver of the action.

Admittedly, there was some skepticism at first. We've all been told that if you're not an officer of the court, there is no way for you to impact a court case. The system is designed to give your loved one "time served"—that's the language the court uses to quantify the amount of time of incarceration. That phrase actually became part of our introduction at the beginning of meetings. We say that by participating in these weekly meetings, you can help turn "time served" into "time saved" for your loved one, meaning they are home, with you, living the life they should be living. We even made the term into a metric to prove the value of community involvement in a case. For example, Lamar was facing a year of jail time for his resisting arrest charge, but through participatory defense, he never set foot into jail. For us, that was one year of "time saved." We accounted for each victory in this way: the amount of jail or prison time someone was faced with versus what they got at the end of the process. This showed that participatory defense amounted to a tangible, identifiable outcome.

Although everyone was fighting against the same system, it was under different circumstances. Some were having their first court date in a couple of days, while others had loved ones who were finally approaching their trial after having been detained for years. Other cases included life without the possibility of parole and still other cases dealt with misdemeanors. No matter the charge or status of the case, there was mutual support every Sunday afternoon.

There is a special bond among people who are in solidarity with one another through the most difficult times of their lives. In this sense, the meetings operated as both support groups for emotional strength and comfort as well as collective strategic planning sessions.

The direct impact on cases was undeniable. We saw charges get dismissed. We saw sentencing enhancements which would have committed a person to die in prison get removed. We saw people that had substance or mental health needs get treatment and care rather than fall deeper into a criminal punishment system that would have only harmed them further. The interventions from participatory defense happened at every point along the timeline of a case. These included winning pretrial freedom at the first court date instead of facing an out-of-reach bail amount, influencing negotiations when a defense attorney was trying to move a prosecutor from a clearly overcharged case, and helping win acquittals in trials. Participatory defense was effective even after a conviction occurred, when a family made a compelling argument that their loved one deserved to be resentenced and returned to the community.

We created a ceremony at our participatory defense meetings—called the "erase the name" celebration—to celebrate our wins. Since we write the names of loved ones on the whiteboard every week, everyone who came regularly would get to know and care about those persons. We would learn about them from their family members, or they might call in during the meeting. For some, given how long court cases could last, the names would be written on the board every week for years. But when the families won—they got the charge dismissed, or the sentence reduced, or won a "not guilty" verdict at trial—those who were facing the charges would attend a meeting in person once they were freed. When their names were called, they would walk up to the board, and instead of someone else writing actions steps on their behalf, they would erase their names themselves. It is a spiritual event. People in the room are clapping, crying, and hugging. Erasing the name means that the community has won. For the new families in the room who are just starting down this road, it lets them know that freedom is possible, that they, too, may be seeing their loved ones erase their names.

Our participatory defense tactics were immediate, identifiable, and doable. No one was trying to be a pseudolawyer; we were just bringing to bear our experience, intelligence, and resources. Families were getting critical defense-related information to the defense attorney—including biographical information—so they knew more about the person besides what was in their case file. Over time, we developed a collective, cumulative intelligence. With every meeting, we learned about different charges, defense strategies, prosecutorial theories, individual judges' biases, the best ways to talk to different types of attorneys, and so much more. A person would come to the meeting not knowing much at all about a loved one's case besides the arrest date. There is no "My Loved One Got Arrested" school, so there's no reason for people to know about the intricacies of the system until they are in its crosshairs. Over time, they would learn what questions to ask, how to find court information and case related documents, and how to ask friends for character letters.

The work in between meetings usually involved providing a fuller picture about a person's life and revealing the devastation incarceration could cause. The most common refrain we would hear from families after a sentence was imposed was "I wish the judge and jury knew them like we do." It meant a court system should have to bear witness to the struggle and challenges the person faced before the alleged incident even happened, and the potential future that awaited. It meant that the court needed to know what was at stake—that the court actors determining the fate of someone should have a bigger, more honest, set of reference points beyond an alleged charge. As organizers, we heard a clear call to action: to create a vehicle for families' stories to provide context to the court about what years in prison would really mean for their loved ones. This meant interrupting the sterility of the court assembly line with real human stories. We called them "social biography packets"—binders of letters, photos, certificates, medical records, any information the family had that framed a deeper, textured narrative of who their loved one was. It is still one of the most used tools of participatory defense for families regardless of the status of the case.

At first, public defenders didn't know what to do when families gave them a social biography packet. In fact, public defenders were initially skeptical about the entire participatory defense approach. They didn't understand why typically empty courtrooms were suddenly being filled by not only their client's family members but other supportive families as well, or why their client's parents were sending information to the defense investigator. Years later, we would learn why public defenders kept their distance from our participatory defense efforts. They worried that family and community involvement would jeopardize their client's case rather than assist it, and that family involvement would take away from their already limited time to work on the case. As time passed, both concerns evaporated, as the participatory defense approach addressed both issues. For example, at our meetings, families learned that jail calls are recorded, so they shouldn't talk about the case on those calls. They learned that approaching the kid who accused a family's son of starting a fight to tell the truth could end up hurting the case, maybe even leading to new charges. As for the concern of attorneys' time being taken away due to family involvement, the reality is that family members who wanted to advocate for their loved one were going to call that attorney every day whether or not they utilized a participatory defense approach. But once that family had a weekly place to find support, share valid emotions, and get answers to basic questions about the court process, their communication with the attorney became laser-focused, time productive, and useful for the case.

The initial dynamic was rooted in a history of distrust between public defenders and the communities they represented in court. This was partly reflective of the way every service, regardless of the field, is valued in America. The "you get what you pay for" mantra also gets applied to legal representation. This means that people assume that scraping together whatever resources you have to hire a private attorney is always better than using a public defender. Yet, the families we work with often ended up returning to a public defender when they could no longer afford a private attorney, even though their family member's case was ongoing. The public defender was also the family's first formal interaction with the courts. That meant it was a public defender who told a family that the bail amount was an exorbitant $50,000, that the gang enhancement charge stemmed from the neighborhood they were from and the color of their skin, and that the "choice" was between a plea offer of five years in prison or a trial where losing would mean a sentence of twenty-five years to life. Public defenders often end up being the bearer of the worst news.

So when families dug their heels into the fight, sometimes it felt like the target sights were set on the public defender. People, justifiably, and regardless of the charge or length of sentence, felt like they were in a David versus Goliath battle of their lives when they or a loved one was facing the court system. They saw themselves as David, righteously protecting their people, but would mistarget the public defender as the Goliath they must bring down.

We learned that they were correct about the enormity of the battle, and that they were in fact David. But Goliath wasn't the public defender; it was the system itself. Goliath was mandatory minimums, prosecutorial compulsions to secure convictions at any cost, and racial bias baked into every aspect of the court process, including the laws themselves. In this reframing, public defenders became the sling and rock David uses to take down the giant. Public defenders could be a weapon of the movement rather than an apparatus of the carceral system.

Of course, this isn't to say that there aren't also bad lawyers, including public defenders, who don't bother to meet their clients in jail, who are disrespectful to families, or who default to forcing plea deals on clients simply so they can move on to the next case. In those instances, families work to hold attorneys accountable by demanding a more robust and attentive defense, thereby bringing a healthy tension to the relationship. Sometimes that concerted, consistent pressure would change an attorney's performance within the life span of a single case.

Roughly eight out of ten people facing charges will be represented by a public defender. Because public defenders tend to be the sole legal advocate for the vast majority of people facing charges, improving public defense is one of the least talked about yet most statistically significant ways to mount a strong fight against incarceration. Public defenders, just like the people they represent, are being asked to play against a stacked deck. The many we have worked with had caseloads that all but ensured they didn't have the time they wanted to fully dig into a case. A public defender would often be the only person in a courtroom fighting against an incarceration, while everyone else—including the judge, prosecutor, and probation officer—was fighting *for* one. I doubt any of them were in law school dreaming of the day they would plea their clients out at 98 percent (which is the plea rate in

Santa Clara County around the time we started). They were being asked to be advocates in a system that forced pretrial detention for those who simply didn't have the money to pay bail. They had to advise a young person facing a gang charge (which is almost exclusively used on Black and Brown people) on whether to take a deal or risk trial when they knew the bias of a jury would make a fair trial highly unlikely. They saw people they knew were innocent take pleas rather than go to trial because they couldn't afford to be away from their family or job any longer. It turned out that the nature of the court system often made public defenders feel isolated and overwhelmed as well.

Over time, public defenders ended up reaching out to us on cases where they could use support. They would refer their clients' family members to our meetings or let us know of upcoming hearings where community presence could be especially important, so that when they and their clients looked back over their shoulders, they would see support in the courtroom pews. In fact, an off-the-cuff statement from Avi Singh, a public defender who works closely with De-Bug families, has become something of a rallying cry for us. He had a client who survived a police shooting and was being wrongfully accused of attempting to hurt the officer who shot him. A few of us from De-Bug had come to watch the trial and were visibly shocked that the man was even being charged. When we were leaving, after everyone had cleared out of the courtroom pews, Avi turned to us, seeming to recognize our shock, and said, "These injustices happen every day in empty courtrooms." For us, that was a call to action to partner with public defenders to fill these courts.

In fact, the title of this book, *Protect Your People*—which has also become our movement's tagline, emblazoned on the shirts we wear walking into court—started as a chant at a march as we sought to bring the energy of mass protests against police violence

15

into the courts. We started the march at the police station and ended at the DA's office about half a mile away, with families belting that phrase over bullhorns. We had two distinct targets: the police and the district attorney. But what unified the efforts was a common purpose—to protect our people against the same systemic threat, whether police abuse in the streets or the continued harms of prosecution and incarceration inflicted through the courts.

What we were doing at these meetings and in the community wasn't an innovation nor was it unique to De-Bug. We were tapping into an instinct, an impulse to fight collectively that already exists in communities who have been targeted by the carceral system. There is a natural community-organizing IQ built from generations of struggle—latent people power that when tapped could make tangible, real, proximate change. What was on display with every case was what happens when that organizing power was mapped on top of a local court system context. And while participatory defense was dramatically impacting case outcomes, what was also undeniable was how people were transformed in their sense of power in the face of a system that was designed to strip them of agency. This was how participatory defense was an articulation of sustained movement building. This community presence and voice was in direct opposition to the isolation of the court decision-making machinery that fueled high-speed incarceration in jurisdictions across the country.

The organizing energy didn't end when a case was resolved. Through participatory defense, people saw their capacity to change a trajectory they were told they couldn't, and they wanted to support other families. Participatory defense becomes an entry point for people who were battle tested through their own intimate fights to get involved in the movement for racial justice around them.

Sharing the Model

From 2006 on, our practice grew in San Jose. We met weekly, became regulars at court, and our families kept working with defense attorneys to free loved ones. More cases meant a continuous expansion of community knowledge about how to push back and beat a potential incarceration, and how collective action could manifest into a campaign, an innovation, a disruption of the punishment system. By 2015, we started sharing the model with people outside of our city. Community groups who had heard about what we were doing asked us to share how the model worked. Public defenders looking to build a connection with the community they represented in court reached out to see if we could start a conversation on what participatory defense might look like in their county. We assumed that something like what we were doing was already happening in cities across the country—and in a lot of ways, it was. Organizing support for those facing the courts is a long-standing tradition, and our work simply followed in this tradition. Participatory defense asserted that the impulse that led community leaders to write character letters or cousins to take up the first three rows of a courtroom for a trial could be sustained and ultimately become a source of support for every person facing court. Instead of being a powerful flashpoint that is raised periodically, it could be a regular practice—a light that never goes out.

Participatory defense practitioners—like Gail, Blanca, Cecilia—became participatory defense trainers. We would go to a city where community groups had asked about starting the organizing model and share the methodology. We would spend a couple of days with a community organization, hearing familiar stories of how policing and incarceration had torn apart their city, and how they were steadfast in their commitment to stop the devastation.

In our initial presentations, we would analogize participatory defense to the tools, metaphorical and literal, that organizations already had to respond to crises. For example, most organizations were equipped with fire extinguishers. Yet no one had a "break glass in case of emergency" tool for the threat of a community member's looming incarceration. We would share participatory defense tactics so other community organizations could be prepared should one of their members catch a case. But some groups said the figurative fires of the carceral system weren't isolated incidents but were, in fact, burning in their communities all the time. They didn't need a fire extinguisher; they needed to become a fire station—a larger, sustaining, infrastructure capable of responding in a more expansive way. These groups would become participatory defense hubs.

For new hubs, our team would share how to get the weekly meetings started, how to make social biography packets and videos, how to read police reports, and how to build relationships with the public defenders. We would look at a timeline of a felony case that laid out all the stages, from arrest to trial to appeal, and share what a participatory defense group could do at each point to intervene and impact the trajectory of the case. Once the groups got up and running, they became a participatory defense hub.

The hubs came in different shapes and forms. Some were justice organizations that worked on police accountability, some were organizations of formerly incarcerated leaders, and others were immigrant rights advocates—but they didn't have to be formalized organizations that were already explicitly fighting against incarceration. Some were youth centers, some were faith-based centers such as churches, and still others were groups of families who met at the training and then created a coalition or collective to build the hub. If the movement to end incarceration was going to effectively take on such an entrenched and powerful system, it needed to cast a wide net—beyond just nonprofits with explicit missions to end incarceration or work on justice reform. The devastation of incarceration was so sprawling, so ubiquitous, that the movement challenging it also needed to be equally expansive.

We realized that the best candidates for participatory defense hubs were groups that flew at the same altitude as De-Bug— meaning close to the ground. They were people or organizations that others turned to in moments of crisis. These types of community touchstones absorbed participatory defense the most fluidly into their natural walk for freedom. We found that this organic organizing infrastructure that could incorporate participatory defense into existing ways of serving and protecting the community was everywhere. It didn't matter if it was a rural county or a big city, whether it had a bunch of nonprofits or not, or whether or not it had a high-profile history of taking to the streets to protest systemic racism. Every jurisdiction where the apparatus of incarceration was operating, separating, and killing was also consequently a place where the firepower required to push back through participatory defense was already brewing.

The incredible people who are part of their respective participatory defense hubs in many ways seem made for this work. They had been targeted or locked up themselves and wanted to prevent that harm from happening to others in their community, so they joined the hub.

In New Orleans, Louisiana, the hub is led by Fox and Rob. Rob served over twenty years in Angola prison, and won a commutation in 2018 thanks to his and Fox's persistence and commitment to his freedom. Their core group of leadership is made up of the families Fox rode the bus with to visit their loved ones in prison, and the men Rob sat next to in bunks in prison, who talked about doing exactly this while they were fighting for their freedom and that of others while in prison. In San Diego, California, the hub is led by Pillars of the Community, a neighborhood-rooted organization that advocates for young Black men falsely targeted for gang crimes. In Philadelphia, Pennsylvania, the first hub in that city is hosted by Mothers in Charge—an organization dedicated to ending gun violence. On the other side of town, the Youth Art & Self-Empowerment Project (YASP) is the first youth-focused hub in the network. In Orange County, California, the hub is housed in the Rapid Response Network, which protects the community from U.S. Immigration and Customs Enforcement (ICE). In Knoxville, Tennessee, there wasn't a preexisting organization; instead, people came together at the first participatory defense training and formed a hub now called the Community Defense of East Tennessee. One of the first hubs we trained in Montgomery County, Pennsylvania, was a service agency that had a program for new fathers. In Boston, Massachusetts, the hub of Families for Justice is led by formerly incarcerated women. A number of the participatory defense hubs were founded by partnering with the National Council of Incarcerated and Formerly Incarcerated Women and Girls. Where they had council sisters, we knew there were movement leaders who could launch a hub and win time saved. We sometimes had to dissolve the false conception that community power could have only limited impact in a court setting. We weren't suggesting a new piece of legislation or an army of new lawyers to protect the community—it was the community itself. Building over eight years, we now have a National Participatory Defense Network of over forty hubs in thirty different cities. Each is growing the practice, and we are all learning from each other in ways that will allow us to advance the work locally.

Three key tenets inform our key values:

1. Family and community strength can play a pivotal role in stopping or limiting the incarceration of a loved one.

2. Families and communities can be more powerful as organizers and change agents than as service recipients.

3. By working on individual cases, communities can build and contribute to movements of directly impacted people to hold court actors accountable, win systemic change, and ultimately end incarceration.

Each of the hubs in the National Participatory Defense Network counts its respective "Time Saved" numbers every year. In this annual tradition, we all gather at the same place we first gathered at our first multihub convening—a small, out-of-the-way beach just south of Santa Cruz. After adding up all the time saved by each hub, we reveal the total years won back as a national collective. Everyone is usually blown away because we each know what it took to win a single year in our respective cities. By the end of 2022, the National Participatory Defense Network had won 25,869 years of time saved from incarceration.

This book shares the stories of participatory defense practitioners from across the country who are paving this pathway to freedom, to time saved. In that way, it is part diary, part guidebook. It is a window into participatory defense hubs, their people, the journeys that brought them to the work, and what they are building. They share their stories as parents, children, partners, and survivors of incarceration. But they also write as history makers, movement builders, and a generation that has found a method and a practice not just to fight for freedom for themselves and their loved ones, but to build a collective future of justice and liberation for all.

Part I

TYPES OF INTERVENTIONS

1

SOCIAL BIOGRAPHIES

We're taught that the criminal legal system is based on empirical evidence, rights, and immutable laws. But ultimately, it's the stories that are told in courtrooms that can make a real difference. And unfortunately, the stories that dominate court hearings are usually told by police and prosecutors. They often construct an entire narrative of who a person is with just a police report, a charge, or a rap sheet. To be the storyteller is to have power in the court process. In the early days of our hub, the place we saw this most clearly was at sentencing hearings.

Once a family member was sentenced to a particularly long prison sentence—ten, twenty, or forty years—we would all walk with the person's mother, son, and/or partner back to the parking lot while they processed what their life would now be like. While often the conversations were about how heartless the judge was, or how vengeful the prosecutor was, their reflections were usually about the story they were forced to hear about their loved one's life. The most common thing people would say was: "We just wish they knew them like we do." In other words, if a court system has the power to take people's freedom and separate them from their families, it should also have the responsibility of truly knowing who those people were, both before the incident they were being judged on, and with respect to the future life that they dreamed of and built toward. The goal of telling the true story of a life was to provide a bigger, more honest set of reference points than the intentionally limited language of the courts could communicate. For this to happen, families needed to become the storytellers. As organizers, this became our clear call to action.

We call them "social biography packets"—packaged binders with a cover photo of the person depicted in a way that speaks most to who they are, a table of contents, and sections organized to tell a coherent story. The binders include handwritten letters, photos, certificates, medical and school records, accomplishments kept in a scrapbook—any information the family has that frames a deeper, textured, narrative of who their loved one is. They are curated into chapters such as "Friend and Family Support," "Future Opportunities," "Prior Challenges Overcome." To piece together and present the life journey of a loved one in order to save that life is a daunting and awesome project. I think that's why families are so rightfully proud when they finish making these packets. It responds to what families had wanted to do since the beginning of an arrest: to share who their loved one is beyond a static allegation. The human rights leader Bryan Stevenson once famously said, "Each of us is more than the worst thing we've ever done," as a way to expose the irrationality of mass incarceration. Social biographies are a practical, real way to share the "more" by those who have the most proximate knowledge— parents, partners, siblings, children, loved ones.

For the defense attorneys receiving them, the social biographies are the personalized material they need to support their arguments to dismiss charges, reduce sentences, or whatever the particular defense goal is. In some ways, attorneys have been asking for social biography packets for years, even if they couldn't articulate it. These requests would usually take place at a hearing before a sentencing, or a rendering of a bail decision, when the attorney would ask a family member to "write a character letter."

Sometimes it was the first conversation the attorney had ever had with the family, who were generally excited that there was something they could do besides just sitting in the court and listening.

But there is no "my loved one got arrested" school. So naturally, family members weren't sure what to write for these "character letters," and would often end up communicating with generalities such as "He is a really good guy," or "Give her another chance." Of course, these types of statements aren't specific or personalized enough to advance the argument of release or undermine the narratives from the prosecutor and police. When the defense attorney and family have an opportunity to collaborate, identifying the key themes that need to be lifted up, they can present a story with strategic value. The family-created social biography packet not only enhances the defense attorney's case, it also brings the case to life. For instance, if the court has concerns about substance use, the family might include a section in the packet about how their loved one's history of working on sobriety had allowed the individual to serve as a guide and mentor to others. If the defense attorney is making the case that a "new start" is needed to get out of a cycle of incarceration, the social biography packets can illustrate opportunities being put in place: a photo of the room in the apartment that awaits the loved one, employment confirmations, and school enrollment acceptance letters.

In the courtroom, sentencing, bail decisions, and charges are mathematic. The legal system considers a charge, assigns a time value to it, and spits out a number of years of incarceration. It's an arbitrary process. Who says twenty years of incarceration is the numeric expression of "justice"? Who says rehabilitation is even a function of time? To fight the system, we needed to take the conversation outside of its made-up math, to force judges and prosecutors to confront the reality that they are making a decision about a dynamic human life, not filling out an equation.

And while the packets are "social" in the sense that they are about locating a lived experience among social and cultural ecologies and environments, these stories are political, and families can decide how explicitly they want these landscapes spelled out. Telling a personal story of housing instability someone faced growing up timelines gentrification in that city. Sharing about the lack of educational opportunities shows how policy makers decided to defund public schools in Black and Brown communities. Prior arrests of a person as a youth can be understood by sharing the disproportionate policing, harassing, and arresting in that under-invested hyperpoliced neighborhood. A family's struggle to find economic opportunities can be understood as the consequence of generations of anti-immigrant policies locking them out of the promised American dream.

These are real, political, seismic, racialized forces and histories that couch an individual story into a larger backdrop that the court system intentionally would otherwise ignore and disassociate. Families and communities can tell these stories, with lived experience and reflection, and present back to the court who the person standing before it is, on their terms.

Over the years, hubs found another effective medium with which to communicate these truths: video.

Social Biography Videos

It started with making celebration videos of a family back together in their home, or a mom at their kid's birthday party after getting released, or an uncle being able to coach his nephew's soccer game instead of being locked up. The videos captured the sights, sounds, and real-time emotion of what freedom looked and felt like in a life story. So we thought, why not do videos for cases that are still being decided? Why not use the medium of video to introduce judges to people's real lives, and bring the reality of communities into the court? They would be video interpretations of the packets. The videos didn't need to be Oscar winning; they just needed to be windows into the rest of a person's story that a letter or still photo couldn't communicate in the same way. They could be made by anyone, using equipment they already had. The footage could be captured on phones and edited on free software.

We would interview someone's mom in the childhood home as she shared the struggles the family went through when they first came to this country. Or we would film a basketball coach at a park talking about his commitment to mentoring a young person once out. One of the first videos we made was for a sentencing hearing of a young man who had overcome tremendous instability at an age when he should have been looked out for by adults. He walked us through the parking lot behind a grocery store where he had to sleep at night when the foster home would kick him out. That visual and the emotion carried in the reflection were best captured on film. That judge may not have ever set foot in that parking lot, but he had to see it, and understand that the young man faced struggles as a teenager that no sentencing scheme would truly account for.

The social biography videos were impactful in the same way as the social biography packets. And for the family members who wanted these court actors to know their loved ones' life stories "like we know them," it allowed them to share in a natural way. Outside of this avenue, another way a lot of people are shoehorned into talking about loved ones facing the courts is as character witnesses in a hearing. This is such an artificial and abnormal setting that it limits what is said and how it is communicated. Testifying is an incredibly daunting task, and the format betrays what its proposed aim is: to hear truth from people. A person is asked to say this truth in a court, with bailiffs and other attorneys with cases watching, and with the possibility of being cross-examined by a prosecutor. But in social biography videos, they are sharing their stories, important reflections, or plans for the future from a place where they feel comfortable, a setting of their making.

The videos can be submitted to the public defenders to use when trying to win bail hearings, or reduce charges, sentences, or win resentencings. The prosecutor or judge may review the video in their offices, but what is always incredibly moving is when they play the videos in open court. They wheel out a projector and screen, press play—and the entire atmosphere of the court changes. This feelingless room—where people would be separated from loved ones, sent to cages, sentenced for years on end with that cold arithmetic—pauses. In this room, children share how their mothers taught them to always be courageous in hardship; partners share how a loved one would prepare all their medicines while they were fighting cancer; parents sit in a backyard reminiscing about the life dreams of their son when he was a young boy.

And oftentimes the person who the video is for had been incarcerated during the making of it, so this is the first time even they were seeing the video. Outside of funerals and eulogies, the reality is there are not too many times people hear from those who love them, talk about them, and share images and stories of what they mean to them.

So after the video is played, and the lights are turned back on, people weep, embrace, take deep exhales as the business of the court attempts to get back in order. It is a necessary intrusion, and often contributes to meeting the goal of a community wanting to share the truth of someone while assisting in the charge, bail, or sentence being reduced or eliminated.

Whether in a video or a packet of photos and letters, families being storytellers has been a sustaining practice of participatory defense through the years. It doesn't really matter where the case is procedurally—early on or after a conviction—the story sharing is always a way for the defense attorney to better know who they are representing, and why their advocacy is so important.

This section shares how families and hubs from across the country created social biographies that stopped prison sentences, eliminated million-dollar bails, lifted charges off of loved ones, stopped deportations, and won commutations and resentencings. Stories—and who is allowed to tell them—can directly change the outcome of a court case, transforming the landscape of power in the courtroom.

San Mateo, California
Don't Just Say It, Show It:
The Social Biography Packet
Charisse Domingo
SAN MATEO HUB

We were a couple of months into our Sunday meetings at De-Bug when we first met Carnell. A young father of three, he'd come in with his girls in tow. They would carry their books, dolls, and arts and crafts. They'd play patiently at the corner of our community center while Carnell would join the group. Despite the heaviness of the tone of the meetings, Carnell would stop what he was doing whenever one of his little girls came up to him. His gears would shift immediately from serious to soft.

Carnell was facing a charge of drug possession for sale that carried a five-year prison sentence. He was arrested for selling $20 worth of drugs to an undercover officer in East Palo Alto. While he admitted to doing so, the five-year sentence remained tough to swallow. At the time of the incident, Carnell was the sole provider for his children, the sole caretaker of his disabled mother, and had been on a steady path of rehabilitating his life since he was released from prison almost ten years prior. He admitted to having a recent stumble with drugs, all the while being able to meet his responsibilities as a father and as a son and was focusing back on his recovery after a momentary lapse. His children's mother had not consistently been in his or the children's lives for years. If Carnell were to be sent to prison, it would mean his children would be sent to the foster care system and his mother possibly being placed under conservatorship left no one to care for them.

Carnell really wanted the judge to know how devastating his imprisonment was going to be for his children. "I can handle the environment itself," he said, "but I don't want my kids to have to go through it." All of us at those Sunday meetings had a clear visual of what that loss could look like. Three little girls who would always hold hands and listen politely to their dad. We couldn't imagine Carnell out of that picture. At every meeting, he would tell the group that he just wanted the judge, the district attorney, his public defender, and the courts to know that he really was a good dad. We all saw it.

Then one Sunday, one of the mothers of our group just said, "Why don't you show it?"

We all paused. Looked at each other. Maybe if the court saw what we saw, then if they handed down a sentence, they'd see those three little girls and the effects of incarceration on them too. And at least take that into account. Plus, Carnell was already working on his recovery. Without prodding from an attorney, friend, or family member, he joined a recovery group for the first time, and had been going faithfully. He understood what was at stake and had already taken steps.

We then gave Carnell two cameras—those disposable ones

that you just point and shoot and that you can buy at a Walgreens. Digital cameras weren't a thing yet, much less iPhones. So we bought him the cameras and gave him an assignment—just take photos of your week with the kids, and you have forty-eight shots to do it. The following week, he came back with the two envelopes of developed pictures, and they revealed a more holistic version of Carnell's life, a repeat of the same tenderness we witnessed at the Sunday meetings. He took photos of breakfast they made together, drives to school, volleyball practice, homework, and bedside reading. There were photos of him taking care of his mother—cooking her food, helping her walk and get dressed. He assembled them like a photo album and proudly showed the group like it was a school presentation. He was joyful, telling stories, and we were eager to see them. As he went over each one, we had another idea—that he write his story down. De-Bug's origins have always been about naming our stories, trusting in their truths, understanding that the sum of our life stories is the sum of various political, social, economic moments that intersected to form the context of how we move through the world.

Carnell grew up in the city of East Palo Alto, California, a place he loved but that didn't love him back. It wasn't always that way. East Palo Alto was created by the Black imagination during the resistance movements of the sixties and seventies. Within 2.5 square miles, they had their own college, health center, schools, community centers, and Black-led government.

They called it Nairobi.

Driving on the 101 Freeway now and exiting University Avenue toward the main vein of East Palo Alto, one would never know that such vibrancy existed. Gone are the "only in East Palo Alto" brick and mortars that were razed to build office buildings. A mixture of the brutal policies that made up the war on drugs in the nineties, the massive redevelopment that excluded East Palo Alto and East Menlo Park, and gentrification physically and spiritually tore down this community. This is the East Palo Alto that Carnell grew up in. His life is a tale of his city. His family was one of the 75 percent of Black people who used to live in this small town carved out of all the wealth of Silicon Valley. East Palo Alto was also once described as the murder capital of the world.

Carnell's first brush with the system was two weeks after his grandmother passed. He was only thirteen years old. He was sitting next to her when she suddenly coughed up a lot of blood and died. Later their family would find out she had been suffering from cancer, but no one knew she was sick. The sudden death of his grandmother, who had been his safe space—the one who took him in when his mother was deep into her addiction and his father wasn't present—changed the trajectory of Carnell's life. Two weeks after her death, unsure of how to deal with his loss and with no adults to guide him through his grief, he was detained by police when he tried to leave after a teacher asked him to stay after school. She had blocked the doorway and he ran under her and pushed by her. He spent a day in juvenile hall for battery on school grounds.

Instead of football fields, or community centers, or high school classrooms—places that should be familiar to teenagers—Carnell walked in and out of juvenile hall, foster homes, the county hospital, California Youth Authority, and later, San Mateo County jail. Drugs numbed the loneliness that appeared as anger. After some time in prison and coming home in 2000, Carnell stayed clean and devoted his life to raising his three girls.

Telling his life story in context of what was happening in the community was not to excuse Carnell's actions, but to add nuance and a sense of history. He didn't see himself as a victim of his environment, but rather a point of intersection within it. Individual choices are affected by historical trajectories and consequences. Naming those forces allowed him to then become an agent of his destiny. He wrote his story to go with his photos. And the actual practice of writing gave him the latitude to reflect and, more important, to forgive himself:

Around 1990, at the age of 15, me and my dad wasn't getting along. So I left and moved in with my aunty. I got in trouble riding in a stolen car with my cousin, stealing and smoking cigarettes. I even got drunk one time to fit in. I didn't like the way alcohol made me feel so I didn't try that again. My stubborn, immature ways caught up with me because I was sent to the boys' ranch called Camp Glenwood in La Honda in 1991 and turned right around and got sent back for riding in a stolen car with my cousin and was charged with car theft. I got kicked out of the boys' ranch. Since it was my second time and I was still feeling alone, my attitude was one of who didn't care. All I could think of is how could God take my granny from me. Me not being able to handle those emotions after witnessing my grandmother pass changed me, especially without any real adult support.

Being in the system put a serious problem on my life later. I started smoking weed and lacing it with cocaine. Just to ease the pain of being lonely.

If it's one thing I've learned, it's easy to do wrong. But hard as ever to do right. Sometimes when you can't put the past behind you. If I could go back and start over, I wish I never spent that one day in juvenile hall. But I learned that God is forgiving. I attend church with my mother and step-mother. I've met new people that show support that barely even know me. Made new friends. Learn how to forgive myself and others. We learn from our mistakes and I make no excuses for my wrongdoings. My immature ways could cost me my daughters. I can be a better example, 'cause my daughters deserve better and so do I.

I wake up with a good attitude as I get my kids dressed and ready for school. Then off to work. After work, I pick my kids up from school. Have them take their baths. Fix them dinner, and help them with homework. I attend all teachers' meetings and been doing so since their first day of school.

I'm very involved in their lives, mainly because I want them to have better chances than I did. Praise them as they involve themselves into new things. Let them know it's okay to dream big. My oldest is 13 years old, and I made the wrong choices at that age. I am a better man today and hoping for a new chance to learn and grow even more. Not just for me but also for the ones that love me the most—my 3 daughters: Amaria, 13; Aniya, 7; and Akeela, 4.

That was the start of what has now evolved to become the "social biography packet"—a collection of letters, photographs, documents, and records that tell a fuller picture of who a person is beyond the case file. None of us knew if it would work or how a judge would receive it. The day at court when he took his plea, Carnell and I were sitting in the courtroom pews unsure of what was going to happen that day. His attorney walks in and tells us he'll be talking to the judge and the prosecutor in chambers. About fifteen to twenty minutes later, the attorney says that the prosecutor didn't want to budge off the maximum exposure, but the judge was willing to consider an open plea—meaning that Carnell would have to plea to the charges, but at sentencing, the judge would consider the max of five years or the minimum of probation. The attorney came over to Carnell and said, "You still working on that 'social bio' thing? We can bring that to court to see if the judge will go for probation after reading it."

Carnell had to decide then.

He turned to me and said, "We gonna do this? I'm gonna take my chances with the judge." He wasn't scared.

For weeks after that, Carnell and our group worked on the social biography packet. He was going to admit to the charges of possession or sale, but the packet would show how he was already taking accountability for his actions, as well as the effects of incarceration on him and his family at this point in time in his life. Even before his sentencing, without any prodding from his attorney or anyone, Carnell himself enrolled in AA classes, joined parenting classes, and found a steady job after months of looking and bouncing around with temp jobs in the Valley. Those were factors that didn't exist during the time of the incident. He and his supporters wanted to show that while he did take responsibility, he belonged in the community, not in prison.

His social biography packet package included:

- Letters of support from his mother, father, stepmother, community organizations and leaders, his pastor, and his children's school counselors, who testified to how vital Carnell was to his kids' lives;
- Certificates of completion and progress in his drug rehabilitation classes and parenting classes;
- High school diploma;

- Paycheck stubs to show that he had consistent work;
- Transcripts of his children's participation and attendance at school that show how, under Carnell's care, the kids did well (getting straight A's, student of the month, participating in after-school programs);
- A photo journal showing how Carnell takes care of his children, from waking them, feeding them breakfast, taking them to school, taking them to volleyball practice, and more.

In preparation for sentencing, a probation officer interviewed Carnell so she could make a recommendation. We figured that this person was an important person to convince that Carnell, his family, and the community would be better served with Carnell home. Knowing when that meeting was gave us our deadline of when the social biography packet would be completed. When he got that date, he brought the social biography packet with him, and walked her through each page of the packet, especially each photo of him and the girls. He left that meeting feeling really positive, a situation that also felt different for him than his previous bouts with system actors who he felt saw him as a checkbox.

I don't even remember if the attorney met with Carnell before sentencing. I just remember that the day of sentencing, Carnell brought three copies of the social biography packet with him. The attorney gave it to the judge and he said the prosecutor wasn't budging on the five years. Carnell brought his friend, another family member, and some of us at De-Bug with him to court. He prepped them on what to do in case he had to be remanded into custody immediately—where the car was parked, what time the kids get out of school, where they were going to stay the night, his keys. All of that.

It was the morning court in San Mateo County. Attorneys bustled in and out. It was mostly continuances, and then people in the courtroom pews just anxiously waiting for their names to be called. You don't ever know if it's their first appearance or their last.

When Carnell's case was called, the prosecutor asked for the full five years, embellishing on Carnell's past history and why it was in the interest of public safety that he be locked up in prison. The judge had Carnell's social bio packet on her dais, and as Carnell's attorney made the plea for an alternative to incarceration, she was turning each page of the social bio packet one by one. The court transcript wouldn't show how much time she took reading through each page, but we could feel the silence. She asked the prosecutor if she had seen the packet. It almost wasn't like a question. It was like a statement—with a tone of incredulity that the prosecutor would still ask for the full five years. On top of that, the probation officer recommended a six-month sentence, modifiable in two months to an outpatient program that allowed him to be in the community to work, be with his children, and work on his sobriety.

That day, the judge went with the probation recommendation and uplifted the social biography packet that Carnell made. She praised him, and also allowed him some time to prepare to get things ready for his daughters and mother for the very short time he would be away at the outpatient program he was required to go to. Everyone was pretty shocked walking out of that courtroom. Carnell couldn't wait to tell the rest of the De-Bug folks, but, more important, he couldn't wait to pick up his daughters from school.

That was the first time we ever used a social biography packet, and now, it has become one of the first "to-do's" we ask of families when their loved one has a charge. We know that seeing a fuller picture of a loved one can truly change the way courts make decisions that affect families and communities.

Nashville, Tennessee
Playing a Video in Court to Reunite a Family
Gicola Lane

FREE HEARTS HUB

When many people think of Nashville—a city which is over 65 percent white—they often think of country music, cowboy hats, and honky-tonks. And indeed, city leaders tend to emphasize that image. But the Black neighborhoods I grew up in were nothing like that Nashville, nor are the groups of people lining the courtrooms, halls, and jail dockets at our courthouse. The number of Black people constantly lining the halls of our courthouse is never a surprise to us—the people who were born and raised here—because we are always reminded of how our racist city and state uphold their racist history.

So many times, in my own life, I've experienced that people showing up for me made a difference. From my Uncle Tim being killed by Nashville Police, to my Mama demanding my freedom from juvenile hall when I was arrested for "loitering," to friends sticking by my side when I was facing charges in Atlanta as a college student: I immediately recognized the value of being a part of someone's village because mine had shown up so many times throughout my life.

One day I was approached at the community center I worked at by a community member who asked if I could come to court with him and explain how he helps me out at the center because he was facing some charges. Without any hesitation I agreed. I went to court that day, stood up, introduced myself, and vouched for him using my "director" title. Little did I know I was doing a form of participatory defense before an official invitation would come across my email a couple of months later. I was one of over forty community organizers and advocates in Nashville who received an invitation from our local public defender's office to Nashville's participatory defense training by Silicon Valley De-Bug. A few of my co-workers at the center also received the email, and when they read it, they said, "Gicola, we have to go!" So, we went to the two-day training and spent hours learning about the criminal legal system and what we could do to intervene and help protect our people in Nashville.

A few months after that, and after we had started our participatory defense meetings, a tragic accident happened in the Wells family. Everybody and they mama was so sad after hearing about what happened with Tia and Tariq. At the end of the summer months, Tariq accidentally shot his daughter Tia after she came home early from her first day of middle school. She snuck into the house quietly and thought she would scare her dad as a prank. He thought someone was trying to break into the home, and he fired a shot that ultimately led to his firstborn child passing away.

Tariq was charged with reckless homicide, possession of a firearm with a felony conviction, and tampering with evidence. By the end of the week of nonstop news stories about the case, #ForeverTia was going viral, as her loving dad sat in the county jail with heavy grief facing up to eighteen years in prison in the state of Tennessee.

My big cousin Kim called me about it because her daughter went to school with Tia, and they were on the cheerleading team together. Kim was heartbroken. She didn't know what participatory defense was, but she knew I did something inside the courts, and she and so many other people just wanted to help the Batts family. Then, my old high-school classmate Christy called me trying to figure out how to get him some support. She knew Tariq from their old neighborhood and was relentlessly trying to get him some help. I let her know all about participatory defense and she hit up his sister, letting her know about our meetings. In the meantime, his family and his friends were already naturally doing participatory defense–style support.

Tariq's bail was ridiculously set at $1 million by the racist judges in Sumner County Criminal Court. Unfortunately this situation is not unique in our state. The bail industry in Tennessee is known to be biased and built on the backs of Black people and cash-strapped communities. I remember attending the bail hearing that day and there were so many supporters for Tariq that they were turning people away. The courtroom was completely packed. The court staff was upset that he had so many people supporting him.

As we filed into the courtroom, the court officers and security were especially rude and strict that day. Regardless of the system and their antics, Tariq's bail was reduced to $500,000, which is still a ridiculous amount. People were so happy that they started cheering and clapping in the courtroom. People busted out in praise like we were all in church! Everyone wanted Tariq home so he and his family could mourn and heal.

One thing I've learned is that the system hates when people celebrate freedom, so the judge quickly started hitting his gavel and yelling out orders to people to remind them of his little authority. Mind you, we were in a county outside of Nashville, where most of us were from. The county we were in, Sumner County, is notoriously harsher, especially on its Black residents, and is governed by all white people. The county is only about 8 percent Black. Later on that day, and following the outpouring of community support for Tariq's family, we ended up raising the $50,000 to pay for the 10 percent of his half-a-million-dollar bail.

Tariq was able to make it to Tia's funeral after his family and community supporters helped bail him out. It was a beautiful service. Tariq wore a tie with pictures of Tia all over it, matching his son and other children. He even unexpectedly spoke at her home-going service. It was a very touching moment.

Not too long after the funeral, everything quickly took a left turn. The Sumner County clerk revoked Tariq's bond, based on some false allegations.

Another thing I have learned is to not just automatically believe the narrative that the state (police, judges, district attorneys) are feeding the public. We see it all the time with police shootings and many of us don't trust that narrative. So why wouldn't it be the same for our people? After Tariq's public support took a hit, my classmate Christy pushed even harder for his family to meet with me about participatory defense. She finally got me connected with them; they were really just trying to pick up the pieces.

Tariq's mother invited me over to her home to meet with her and their immediate family. It was a Sunday afternoon and she had made a meal for everyone. She scheduled the meeting around the time that she knew Tariq would be giving her a call. We all huddled together in a circle around the living room waiting on his call, and right there in her living room in North Nashville, Tariq's family began their participatory defense journey. I asked about all the updates on the case, and Tariq provided them over speaker-phone, with his closest family members chiming in. The number one priority was to figure out how to replace his current attorney because they felt that he was not getting the type of defense he deserved. I ended the night by texting the updates and to-do list to Tariq's mother.

Every Tuesday after that, she would come to our Free Hearts weekly participatory defense meetings with other families who were going through the court system like she was. Eventually she started inviting others to our hub, including her sister and another friend who were both seeking help with postconviction relief for their sons.

Tariq and his family were able to hire a new defense attorney, Joy, a badass Black woman attorney, who is one of the few attorneys I admired for not being afraid to tell it like it is in court. She brought in two other attorneys to the defense team, including Derrick, a Black man who commands attention when he walks through the courtroom. It was good to see that Tariq's attorneys cared about him in a totally different way than his first attorney, who was basically indifferent.

Our hub made sure to honor Tariq and his family's wishes by helping them track communication with Joy, and I told them about the powerful tool of social biography videos. One of the things we really wanted to do was to change the narrative from who Tariq *was* to who Tariq *is*. He hadn't been in trouble for ten years, and we wanted to home in on that. Ten years is a big deal. The district attorney was trying to paint a convenient picture to get a conviction: that Tariq was a drug dealer and a thug. But in reality, his life was being home with his kids and wife. That's what we really wanted to show in the video because we knew it wouldn't be brought up anywhere else in court. We wanted to show ten years of a family man.

That's where we thought the social biography video could really help—through the stories of family members, their pictures, their home videos spliced in, all told in familiar settings. A few months back, De-Bug had trained members from the participatory defense movement on making social biography videos, so core members from our Nashville hub came back home with fresh skills and the resources to put together our very first social bio video for Tariq.

We sat down and thought about themes with his mom and who could really speak about those themes: his fatherhood, his support, and his prospects. We wanted to get Mom on the video for sure. This was the very first video we did after we went to the social bio video training. His mom was really the one who quarterbacked it—she knew who would be willing to speak on Tariq's behalf, scheduled it, and filmed it. I didn't have filming experience but simply put the camera on the tripod and pressed start. That's all I knew how to do, and another member helped with the editing. Every week we worked with his mother on the narrative, theme, content, and interviews for the video.

I was super nervous the attorney wouldn't want to use the social biography video. While it's more widely used now, back then, the social biography video was not really a tool that was used in the courts. So I thought about how we were going to present it so that she could keep an open mind. I went to the De-Bug website where there was a page on social biography videos. It used to have quotes from people who used or saw these videos, including attorneys and judges. I copied and pasted those quotes and emailed them to Joy. I told her that these were examples of people who have used the videos and appreciated the help of the participatory defense hub. I also brought up that we could show it to the community to regain their support if that was appropriate. And she agreed.

Tariq's trial started in at the beginning of the summer. Every day, the family and the support community through the participatory defense hub would circle up in prayer before trial. We would encourage everyone to take notes on whatever stood out to them. When we had breaks, we would debrief and cross-reference notes, then send them to the attorney. We would observe the jury and their reactions. Most important, the notes served as encouragement and moral support to the family. There was so much anxiety for the family, and it's sad because it was their first time seeing him in person after he was locked up.

After three days, the trial resulted in a hung jury: they couldn't reach a verdict on the reckless homicide but found him guilty of unlawful possession of a firearm by a convicted felon and not guilty of tampering with evidence. The district attorney and the defense team ended up agreeing to not retry the case, but that still left Tariq facing up to five years in prison. That's when we sent the final social biography video to Joy. After watching it, Joy emailed and said she loved the video. She said, "Download it, and bring it to court."

At sentencing, Joy started her arguments by introducing the video, and had a big screen set up ready to show it. The judge asked for an offer of proof of what the video was about, and that's when Joy called me to the stand. I was surprised because that wasn't planned, but ultimately I agreed, reminding myself of our commitment to protect our people!

I got sworn in, and Joy asked me who I was, what I did, and my relationship to Tariq and his family. I told them about participatory defense and what we did as a hub. Then the judge asked me about the purpose of the video and I started to address what the prosecutors had said about Tariq, how in their opening statements they kept talking about his past, but that this was about how he had changed. I said the video had interviews of people who know him outside of just this case.

They played our eleven-minute video in court as Tariq wept. It was his first time seeing the social biography video. Right after that, he got up to read a letter he wrote; it was so well put together. He talked about how there was no greater punishment than what he's already going through—which is living a life without his first-born, Tia.

He was sentenced to what amounted to a year. Because of his credits, he was able to come home a little after the beginning of the New Year. When he came home, really the most important thing was that the children and Tariq finally actually got to grieve together. Tia's siblings were the ones really going through it—it was hard to go to school, missing their sister, and they just really needed their dad. The harm that the system put on Tariq and his family was most manifested in taking their mourning process away from them.

And now, five years later, Tariq is home with his family, working hard as a truck driver. His mom continues to be involved with Free Hearts, bringing other families to the meetings and coming with us to the state capitol to push for laws.

The family still goes to Tia's grave every holiday and every birthday to spend time with her. Last Christmas, they took a picture in which everyone had shirts with everyone's relationship to Tia—like one for Tariq that said "Tia's Dad," and one for a sister that said "Tia's Middle Sister," and then one for Tia that said "The Angel." They're able to grieve and process together because Tariq is home. When Tariq came to a Free Hearts event, everyone was really happy to see him home. It's one thing to see people through social biography packets, videos, and in court, but to see them home with family and in community is a full-circle moment.

Our experience with Tariq really showed us how to walk with

a family and each other, especially in such dark moments in their lives. Participatory defense was the window, the invitation, for us to do it.

Philadelphia, Pennsylvania
Preventing Violence in the Streets and Protecting Freedom in the Courts
Robert Blair and Dr. Dorothy Johnson-Speight

BEST OUTCOMES HUB

On a cold, snowy night, almost like a blizzard in Philadelphia, in March 2018, Mothers in Charge held its first participatory defense meeting. We didn't know what to expect from our very new initiative, one whose goal was to support individuals and families in Philadelphia that are caught up in the criminal justice system. This was especially true since, for many years, Mothers in Charge has advocated for families who have been impacted by crime and violence. Mothers in Charge was founded in 2003 by Dr. Dorothy Johnson-Speight, whose son was murdered over a parking space. However, Johnson-Speight was well aware of the judicial system and its unjust way of impacting communities of color.

We were starting this new hub after seeing De-Bug members share about the participatory defense model. Several of our volunteers attended this presentation and had their own experiences of bearing witness to the impact of the criminal legal system in Philadelphia. We all left believing that this was something we wanted to be a part of. In fact, one of our members, Steve Austin, left the presentation saying, and continues to say, "Participatory defense is revolutionary."

As we got closer to the meeting time, our conference room

began to fill, first with our staff and volunteers and then with several members of the community seeking information about and support for criminal charges. Despite the weather, we had a packed house. Our participatory defense hub began with three identified core leaders: Robert Blair, Valerie Todd, and Steve Austin. Each one had enormous amounts of experience with the judicial system, which was a plus for us. Robert Blair had served a life sentence in California with a total of forty years inside before being released for two crimes he did not commit. Steve Austin went to prison at the age of sixteen in the state of Pennsylvania. He went in with a sentence of "Life Without the Possibility of Parole" but was released after serving forty-two years. While in prison Steve Austin won several lawsuits against the Pennsylvania Department of Corrections regarding prison conditions; therefore, he became our go-to guy in providing procedural information. Steve was released from prison at age fifty-eight following a U.S. Supreme Court decision that stated that it was unconstitutional to sentence juveniles to life in prison. Our other facilitator, Valerie Todd, also had years of experience with the criminal legal systems. These three were instrumental in getting the first Mothers in Charge hub up and running. We called our hub Best Outcomes. Valerie would start every meeting by saying "Today is a wonderful day to be alive." It was remarkable how much that simple encouraging reflection meant to the families facing the court system.

The community education and support for participatory defense from the very beginning gave us astounding results both in the community and in the courtroom. Jonathan was one of the first people to bring his case to the Best Outcomes hub. He had been sentenced to three to six years and was to report for induction to prison in thirty days. His attorney was reluctant to file a motion for reconsideration of his sentence, so Steve Austin stepped up to help Jonathan with his submission in reconsideration of sentence. Dr. Dorothy got in touch with the Boston hub and requested information on a bill that they were working on for nonviolent offenders called the "Caretakers Bill." The legislation identified the impact of incarceration on children who would be left behind if a parent went to prison, and asserted that this incredible harm must be considered in sentencing. We wrote a letter, as a hub—leaning on the arguments of the Caretakers Bill—that was tailored to Jonathan as the sole caretaker of his two young sons. On the day he was to report to prison, we were back on the docket for reconsideration.

We filled the courtroom that day with family and community representation from our hub along with strong character witnesses as to who Jonathan was in the community. And on that day, the judge reversed the prison order and placed him on house arrest. That was just one of the major wins for the Best Outcomes hub. Jonathan is now one of the core leaders for our hub, helping other individuals and families win their freedom.

DeVonté Douglass was one of our new participatory defense facilitators who became a core leader like Jonathan. He was arrested for homicide after someone attempted to rob him in his community. After a lengthy investigation into the shooting, the homicide charges were dropped but he was charged with several other allegations. Best Outcomes showed up in the courtroom for DeVonté and submitted a social biography video; he received a year of nonreporting probation, yet another best outcome. DeVonté has gone on to become an integral leader of participatory defense for the city of Philadelphia, as there is now a citywide network of eight hubs across the city. DeVonté helps coordinate court attendance throughout the participatory defense network. Here is DeVonté's story.

Philadelphia, Pennsylvania
Surrounded and Saved by Community Care
DeVonté Douglass

BEST OUTCOMES HUB

Since August 2019, I've been co-facilitating Best Outcomes at Mothers in Charge, Philadelphia's first participatory defense hub. From mid-October 2020 to the end of 2021, I took turns supporting participants and receiving support when I too became ensnared by the criminal legal system.

In the fall of 2020, the Office of the Attorney General (AG) charged me with homicide and affiliated charges. In February 2021, the attorney general's office announced that after a thorough investigation, it was determined I acted in self-defense, so my homicide charge was dropped. I was, however, charged with related, lesser allegations.

On October 13, 2021, I arrived at Philly's municipal court where I'd gone so many times before to support others, but now I was the defendant standing trial. However, as Judge Martin Coleman, who presided over the case, exclaimed, the AG was "a no-call and no-show." When the trial was rescheduled for November 4th, the AG stood me up a second time and, once again, did not alert the court beforehand. At this point, Judge Coleman dismissed the case due to a lack of prosecution. I thought the nightmare was over, but five days later the AG's office refiled charges against me. It claimed that it had not been notified either time of the new court dates.

Fellow organizer Martha Williams suggested we ask a partner hub, the Youth Art & Self-Empowerment Project—a Philadelphia-based organization that was working to create a world without youth incarceration—to do a social biography video. I wasn't sure if they would, because I was older than their typical member, but they enthusiastically agreed. We interviewed my mother, my sister, my brother-in-law, Mr. Robert Blair from Mothers in Charge, and Martha Williams—all people who knew who I truly was.

The social biography video was exciting to make because I got to tell my story, but it did get emotional. I begin to cry at certain points. This was a really moving time, because I had an excellent support team, attorney, and a great crew to help me. I was a part of something that some individuals usually aren't a part of—a community documenting its care for you—and I thank God for that and my support team and everyone involved.

On December 16, my third trial date before it was continued again, sixteen members of Philadelphia's participatory defense network packed the courtroom on my behalf. Prosecutors covered their mics but could be heard commenting on the number of supporters. I came expecting to plead guilty to one of the misdemeanors, but the AG still had the other charges on the table.

This is when my heart started pounding. My attorney Shaka Johnson asked to speak to the deputy AG in the hallway, and the judge allowed it with no comment. She told me I could step back, and I took a seat in the gallery and tried to collect myself, while my fate was being decided just a few feet away. My attorney's advocacy resulted in a dramatically lesser sentence than what they were originally offering me: one year of nonreporting probation.

The one year of probation was because of the social bio video and the support that the deputy attorney general heard was in the courtroom. She saw that participatory defense and my attorney was not backing down from the challenge.

My fifteen-month battle with the criminal justice system,

from which I emerged with six years saved, truly highlights the participatory defense movement's revolutionary power. The letters of support, my attorney, hub meetings that sometimes ran overtime, hub members who dressed to the nines and showed up for me in court, and especially the moving social bio video brought the system's assembly line to a screeching halt and forced court officials to acknowledge not just my humanity, but theirs as well.

2

COMMUNITY EXPERTS

The community occupying the courts is a visceral, undeniable flex of people power. You can feel the atmosphere in a cold courtroom change when it's filled with the community. It means something for those facing the apparatus of the court to look over their shoulder and know they are not alone, and for judges to look up from the bench and see rows packed with supporters of the person whose fate they are deciding.

But the power is not only in the physical presence of a crowded court; it is also held in the knowledge and intelligence that the community brings into the court process. If the community could expand its role from audience members watching the story play out in the court to advocates able to navigate and shape that story, we could change the ending of that story. It's totally appropriate for community knowledge to interject, edit, and refute what court actors tell each other and presume as truth. These stories, after all, are in the end *about* the community—the neighborhoods, histories, cultures. Who then is more of an "expert" on community lives than community members themselves? As such, the infusion of community knowledge to a defense strategy could lay bare the lies and assumptions of a prosecutor's depiction of the person they are trying to incarcerate.

There is a saying from a South Asian philosopher, Krishnamurti, that we often repeat at De-Bug: "You can't get wet by

talking about water." It's just another way of saying that sometimes to truly understand something, you have to experience it.
In court, we heard a lot of lawyers and court-certified "experts"
talking about a community they never experienced—and that expertise was a basis to justify a prison sentence.

The exclusionary culture of the court system meant that
it was allowed its own interpretations of the communities it
was passing judgment on, while being shielded from the truths
of those communities. In courtrooms, an entire neighborhood could be labeled a gang hotspot, a young person's cloth-
ing choice could "confirm" his gang membership, a rapper's
lyrics could be deemed a criminal threat. The gang labeling
in particular carried significant sentencing consequences.
Called a "gang enhancement," this designation could increase
a prison sentence by seven years, ten years, or even make it a
life-in-prison commitment. This possibility changed the cal-
culus when people were deciding to take a case to trial or not.
Going into trial with a gang enhancement meant not only ex-
ponentially more time in prison if convicted but also that the
jury could hold a bias against the person from the very beginning. Calling someone a "gang member" before a conservative,
mainly white jury pool was equivalent to labeling a person a
"terrorist" and still expecting a fair trial.

How a court concluded that someone warranted a gang enhancement was ridiculous. It was based on an "expert" who
was almost always a police officer or retired law enforcement
officer who had taken a class on gangs somewhere along their
career path. Invariably, after being accepted as an expert by the
court, when asked if the person of color in shackles in front of
them facing charges was a gang member who committed the alleged criminal act for the benefit of the gang, the answer was
always yes—based on their teachings and trainings (which could

literally be just a few hours in some class taught by another law enforcement agent).

An example of a particularly egregious use of police "experts" in a court case was for a family we were supporting in San Mateo County. Doug Fort was a De-Bug member who brought the family of his childhood friend to our weekly meetings. His childhood friend was facing years in prison after being falsely accused of being a leader of a crime syndicate. Doug was sitting with the rest of the supporters in court. The gang "expert" was a former police detective. From the stand, when asked by the prosecutor to identify gang members the person facing trial associated with, he looked in the audience and pointed to and named Doug. Doug had been a long-standing community leader and youth advocate in East Palo Alto. Like many authentic and respected leaders, Doug had been through the struggles of being a young Black man in East Palo Alto while growing up. That was one of the cornerstone reasons young people listened to him and sought counsel from him—because he'd been through it. He may have even identified as gang-related when he was a youth, but today, years later, he wasn't a gang member. He was actually running for city council at the time. But the police officer was allowed to make this accusation with the weight and venom of a court-qualified expert.

As inept as the officer was who was elevated as a gang expert, his idiocy also illuminated who real experts were: the community itself who knew most naturally about its neighborhoods, culture, and city histories. Even though he wasn't in a gang, Doug knew more about the neighborhoods that raised him, the youth who lived there, which crews no longer existed, and so on—way more the any police officer who took a class on gangs would. Doug came from these communities, worked in them, and was still a part of them.

So we reclaimed the "expert" label. Doug began talking to defense attorneys to explain how police misidentified neighborhoods in East Palo Alto as gang-related, how what was labeled a criminal enterprise was really kids trying to start a music label, or how a tattoo with a street name was about taking pride in where you're from—nothing more.

Doug spoke with such a deep knowing that he frequently started being entered as a gang expert by the defense attorneys for trials whenever someone was facing a gang allegation. Now we had a countervoice to the police and prosecutors, with the only real authority needed to back it up: lived experience. Having a valid expert explain, give context, and deconstruct falsehoods to juries had immediate impact. Prosecutors had to remove gang enhancements, people won acquittals at trial, and the fictitious racist narratives lost their power and control. Doug now works on cases across the country and has contributed to countless years of Time Saved—all through allowing the truth of his community knowledge to penetrate and occupy space in court deliberations.

Over time, after Doug's breakthrough, community experts became a common feature of participatory defense. This didn't mean that every case required a community expert testifying in court. Sometimes it meant giving defense attorneys background info or the right lens through which to analyze a police report. Sometimes it meant literally taking a public defender investigator to a neighborhood to explain an innocuous graffiti tag that was being used to lock up a child. Once, our hub submitted a declaration based on the request from a public defender representing a man who was facing a trial for a resisting-arrest charge. She asked us to share why communities of color would rightfully be fearful of any police interaction in our city.

In real and directly applicable ways, the community has

invaluable experiential knowledge and intelligence that can challenge a prosecutor's theory, a charge, or a sentence. In the courts, what constitutes an "expert" is dictated by who they want or expect to be that authoritative voice. But what participatory defense asserts is that lived experience is the ultimate authority, and the fictional constructed narratives of the system cannot stand in the face of that truth.

This section details examples of how families and hubs from across the country worked to provide community expertise based on the authority of their lived experience. These stories illustrate not only how community experts can change the perception of someone facing court, but also how an entire community can reclaim its history, its truth, and its identity in the face of a court system that has minimized, reduced, and fictionalized in order to incarcerate. And as you'll see, this redefinition can absolutely change the fate of court cases.

Fresno, California
Challenging Gang Charges with Community Truths
Marcel Woodruff

FRESNO BOYS AND MEN OF COLOR HUB

Fresno, California, which is located directly in the center of the state, has heralded itself as a law and order town that prides itself on the "Hook 'em and Book 'em" approach. As a result of this philosophy, many residents found themselves the victims of the collateral damage of overpolicing. Our city has the highest rate of concentrated poverty in the nation and also a punishing court system. At a deeper level, our local criminal justice apparatus has become a carceral trap for many people of color who are arrested with weak cause and left to fend for themselves in court. So when a group of young men from Fresno Boys and Men of Color attended a statewide gathering in 2017, we went looking for strategies we could implement back home. We heard Jesse Ornelas, a community leader from Merced, speaking about a model called participatory defense, and when we approached him, he assured us that if we learned more about it, we would find it empowering.

The conversation with Jesse marked the beginning of our participatory defense journey, which included a year-long research effort. Ultimately, we became determined to use it to help our loved ones and community members during court proceedings, and to see if we could get policy moved around gang enhancements in our work around district attorney accountability. It took our group close to a year to get everything in order, but in 2018 we launched a six-person team and officially joined the National Participatory Defense Network. For two years, our hub supported families of loved ones who had been charged with criminal offenses and helped to save over thirty years of potential incarceration time while building relationships with various public defenders and defense attorneys in our area.

In the summer of 2020, toward the beginning of the COVID-19 pandemic, our work unpredictably grew in scale. Several defense attorneys noted early on in our relationship that our team held a deep understanding of gangs and gang cultures. It became commonplace for them to consult with me or my team in cases involving gang members. Whether or not our team was directly supporting the family involved or attorneys involved, attorneys would consult us on cases with potential gang enhancements. The working relationship between the groups was a wonderful and empowering experience for both parties.

Then one day we were asked to sit in on a preliminary hearing in which a "gang expert" from the police department was scheduled to give testimony. This is the moment that radically shifted our strategy as a team moving forward.

We arrived early at court, observed the back and forth as the prosecution and the defense waded through the discovery; then the officer took the stand. The first question asked of the officer was "What qualifies you as a gang expert?" and she responded by stating, "I did a two-week gang module in the academy, and I have been on the special gang task force for four months." My team and I were floored at the response and equally alarmed by her depiction of gangs and gang culture that followed through questioning. Most of my team and I have either been involved in or lived in close proximity to gangs for our entire lives. We intimately understood the struggles, the pressures, and the trauma associated with gang life in a way that the law enforcement officer would never be able to. We watched her mispronounce gang names, reduce members to their social media posts, and ultimately reveal her inability to truly see them as human beings.

We debriefed with the defense attorney afterward, asserted that we knew far more than the expert, and suggested that she consider qualifying us as gang experts. She agreed, and in the summer of 2021, I was tapped to support as a potential gang expert during the court proceedings.

During the spring of 2020, the city of Fresno saw a sharp increase in gun violence. One incident involved a drive-by shooting in which a four-year-old little girl was wounded. The severe and sensitive nature of the incident was a prime opportunity for prosecutors to enact their law-and-order tough-on-crime approach and push for life sentences for all the alleged offenders. The attack was alleged to have been conducted by a gang who traveled to a rival gang's territory and carried out an assault while a child's birthday party was happening nearby. One of the defendants, a teenage male, was reported to have been in the car at the time of the assault, and was identified as a member of the gang in question. If tried as an adult, the young man would face a sentence of forty years to life. Our team committed to support him, and for nine months, we worked with the young man's family to learn his history and conducted interviews with his gang, rival gangs, and community members. We built a report based upon what we learned and on our expertise of gangs and gang culture and submitted it to the court.

Through our participatory defense training, we had learned to construct social biography packets. These packets organize stories, images, and accomplishments and are an effective tool to humanize defendants amidst a system designed to solely vilify them. In this case, we adjusted the social bio packet and presented it as a narrative with some clinical assessments that measured proclivity for violence and aptitude for redirection. It also included a diversion plan that integrated an action plan to work with the young man postincarceration. The report was accepted by the courts and the prosecutor offered a few complaints, which forced us to spend two weeks making adjustments. Once everything had been accepted, the transfer hearing was scheduled. The young man was facing transfer from the juvenile court system to the adult court, where he could face a life sentence. If the judge decided against the DA's request to try him as an adult, he would be adjudicated as a juvenile and would face significantly less time. Our next step was to qualify me as a gang expert by the courts so that I could take the stand to elaborate on the report we created.

To be qualified as an expert, I had to formally present my credentials to the court through a resume. It included my lectures, writings, workshops, and trainings and all my years of experience working with gangs and gang members. The defense attorney on the case supported me in crafting it and briefed me on how to present it in the court. When I arrived at court, the young man's grandmother was there and became defensive when I told her that I was the gang expert. She had only seen law enforcement serve as experts in her lifetime. I assured her I wasn't law enforcement, and the young man's mother interjected, saying I was there to explain their world to the courts, and I could be trusted. After I presented my credentials, the motion was made for me to be accepted by the courts as a gang expert, and the judge granted it.

I was on the stand for nearly two hours. The defense attorney asked questions about the report I had created as part of the social bio packet, and the prosecution cross-examined me, trying to poke holes in my logic and my report. I remember being anxious, and the atmosphere was really tense, but I felt confident. I knew that I had a level of understanding and insight that the courtroom needed. It felt liberating and empowering to speak of the community's truth in a space that often makes us feel voiceless and powerless. The climactic part of the testimony came as I was being cross-examined. As the prosecutor questioned me, I noticed a subtle shift in his strategy and logic. At first, the defendant was depicted as a monstrous, gang-banging deviant who was a terror to himself and to those around him. However, the prosecutor's arguments began to soften, and he started to acknowledge the young man as a child, a victim of circumstance, and as vulnerable. He angled these arguments to make the defendant seem impressionable and easily dictated to as justification for hard punishment. I knew as I heard his characterizations shift that my expertise had led him to seeing the young man as a human instead of a terrorist. Something had registered for him, and I was confident the judge had registered that sentiment as well.

Finally, I was dismissed and left feeling a little shaken but confident. I knew that next time, I would prepare for the cross-examination a little more with the lawyer, but I relied on my own expertise and knew that they needed to hear what I knew. I was confident that what I told them expanded their understanding. Two days after my testimony, I left for a vacation in Ghana with word that the judge would render her decision within three weeks. Two weeks later, I was tagged on a post on Facebook by the defense attorney indicating that her client would not be referred to adult court and would instead plea and be sentenced to a mandatory minimum of two years in the juvenile detention facility. The young man's story, his unproblematic nature during incarceration, and a rock-star defense attorney had afforded him a second chance, and in two years, he would come and work with my organization. My organization and I were thanked especially for our work serving as agents who could show the humanity of people to the court.

Our hub in Fresno was excited to break ground on a new front when it comes to challenging the inequities and punitive nature of the justice system. Since our first gang expert case, we have been contracted for six more at the time of this writing. Currently, our goal is to establish a gang expert credentialing service that leverages the participatory defense strategy. Moving forward, our vision is to continue to support families whose loved ones are charged with a crime and develop experts from within the community to offer our expertise during trial proceedings as well.

Philadelphia, Pennsylvania
Solitary Confinement Behind Enemy Lines
Andre Simms

CIRCLE OF HOPE CHURCH SOUTH PHILLY HUB

There was a young man behind enemy lines. His family called him Fats but the judge called him a criminal.

Fats was originally arrested and held on murder charges, accused of killing a cop's son. As one would imagine, these types of allegations brought a frenzy of media coverage and a host of enemies within law enforcement. Fats fought those charges for over three years. Finally, he was found not guilty at the conclusion of a weeklong trial. Most people who are found not guilty of the crimes they were being held for are released and return to their communities to begin rebuilding their life. When you are found not guilty of the murder of a police officer's family member, however, the system works a little differently.

On the second day of trial, while Fats was being transported to court, prison guards conducted an investigative search on his cell. During this search, a cell phone was discovered underneath Fats's cellmate's mattress. Upon his arrival back at State Road prison, Fats was immediately thrown in the hole, where he served over a year in solitary confinement. Fats was later charged in criminal court for possession of contraband, misuse of a telecommunications device, and possession of instruments of escape. As scary as these charges sound, they are all misdemeanors. Most people charged with misdemeanors are given bail, if they're even held in the first place, and eventually get off with probation, community service, or a fine. But when you're found not guilty of the murder of a police officer's son, the system works a little differently.

Fats was denied bail and remained in jail after beating the case that had warranted his arrest in the first place. Not only was this twenty-two-year-old kid held hostage as retaliation, but they charged him with two more jailhouse cases. Although he was not guilty of the original charge, he wasn't celebrating freedom at home. He was facing up to six more years in prison.

As his mother told me of her son's struggle at our participatory defense meetings, I couldn't help but flash back to my not-so-distant days behind bars. I knew all too well the consequences of having your case in the news. Guards from other parts of the jail used to visit my cell "just to see the superstar."

"He doesn't look so tough now, does he?"

Their taunts echoed in the depths of my consciousness. I could only imagine the torture Fats was experiencing in there.

I remembered what it was like to be a kid in an adult prison. The first advice I received upon arrival was to sharpen my toothbrush. I remembered all of the fights, stabbings, lockdowns, many of them over phones. Solitary confinement was torture. In prison, comfort is contraband. Surviving is the real infraction.

I remembered my own jailhouse charges. They offered me jail time, but I'd already done my time. Double jeopardy should've applied, but it didn't. When I fired my lawyer, they called me a fool. When I represented myself, they thought I was crazy. But when I negotiated my freedom, everything changed.

I've been in and out of court my entire life, and each time, there were three or more white people talking about me in front of me as if my voice wasn't worth anything. It wasn't until I decided that my voice needed to be heard that they started listening. I'll never forget how understanding and accommodating the DA was when she had to speak to me directly, compared to how she talked about me when she addressed my former lawyer or the judge. And so when my hub went to California to meet with other participatory defense hubs from across the country to talk through how to get more community experts seen and heard in the courts, chills ran through my body. This would be game changing.

I was thousands of miles away from Fats, but he was who I knew this approach could work for.

When the call came to gather support for his court date, I was more than ready. There was a young man behind enemy lines. There were so many of us behind enemy lines, but if I could do something to help just one it would make those 2,935 days that I spent in a cell much more meaningful. So when Fats's mom asked if I'd offer expert testimony at his sentencing, I told her I would. I stayed up all night preparing my resume for the lawyer. I spent hours creating a list of questions that I anticipated the prosecutor would counter with and more hours answering those questions.

On the morning of the hearing, I woke up early to meditate and affirm with the Creator. I decided to wear a suit, to reflect how I knew an expert looked in the eyes of the adversary. Battles are psychological. On the drive down to court, I practiced answering the questions I'd prepared, even though I've been preparing for this most of my life. My heart began to pound when I entered the courthouse. I was greeted in the hallway by the South Philly hub and all of Fats's supporters. When I saw how many people had shown up for Fats, for freedom, for justice, I couldn't help feeling powerful. We had an army behind us.

I met with the lawyer representing Fats before the proceedings. I shook his hand and delivered to him a folder containing my resume and the other materials I had prepared. He was surprised. Jokingly, he said I was more prepared than he was. I didn't get the joke. As he shuffled through the documents, I explained the plan to him. He was to present me as an expert witness on conditions of confinement, citing my resume and history of incarceration to qualify me as an expert. In the event that the judge refused to admit me as an expert, he was to motion to proffer my testimony as a way to get it on record and before the judge anyway. He seemed to understand, and we proceeded to the courtroom.

As I waited for Fats's case to be called, I observed the judge. He was a temperamental, older white man who seemed to get his rocks off by telling people "No." By looking in his eyes, I could tell he'd been under the influence of power for longer than I'd been alive. It was like watching an addict indulge. He must've felt like God with that gavel, but he wasn't God. He just pretended to be. I knew this to be true. So did he. But I wanted him to know that I knew and so I stared into his soul until I was called to the stand.

There was a young man behind enemy lines. So when I was called to testify on his behalf, I did not flinch. I was asked to raise my right hand and swear. I affirmed. I was asked to state my full name and spell my last name. I obliged. I was asked if I knew Fats personally. I admitted that I did not. The prosecutor objected.

"Relevance. Your honor, this character witness does not even know the defendant."

Fats's lawyer didn't even attempt to introduce me as an expert. What was the point of us speaking beforehand if this guy was just going to get nervous and forget the plan?

I was asked why I came forward to testify. I explained that I worked for the Youth Art & Self-Empowerment Project and we ran a participatory defense hub where we support young people who've been impacted by the criminal legal system. I told the judge about how we've been conducting art and poetry workshops in the Philadelphia jails since 2006. I talked about my work with Temple and Villanova universities. I knew this was a language they'd understand. I name-dropped one organization after another, title after title until I knew the judge was convinced. That's when I explained that I had served eight years in prison at the age of seventeen and that I spent the majority of them in and out of solitary confinement. This combination of knowledge and experience qualifies me as an expert on conditions of confinement.

The room grew quiet as the judge contemplated. He was more curious than anything and seemed genuinely entertained by the idea of a community expert. After what felt like hours of silence, he grunted and said, "I'll hear what he has to say." And hear he did. The lawyer found his nerve and began reading through some of the questions I had prepared.

One point of contention was whether or not Fats was justified in possessing a cell phone. The warden of the jail took the stand before me and claimed that anyone in possession of a cell phone while in jail was most likely using the device to escape or organize criminal activity. He said there were plenty of phones on the block that residents had access to at will. I explained that this wasn't accurate.

There were usually between eight and sixteen phones on a block that housed over a hundred people. Most fights in State Road prison were over the control of the phones. A young kid like Fats wouldn't have a chance to call home regularly without going to war.

Another point of contention was whether Fats was significantly punished for his infractions after spending years in solitary confinement. That same prison official suggested that since a portion of that time in solitary was technically under what's called "administrative confinement," he was not necessarily being punished. This too was inaccurate.

I shared that in my experience the difference between administrative confinement and disciplinary confinement was the paperwork that had been filed. To administrators, it's a different housing status, but that person on administrative confinement is still on a twenty-three-hour lockdown. They get to leave their cells only to shower, and during the time Fats was in solitary, the heightened COVID precautions would have made his time even more punitive.

The prosecutor grew red with frustration. Even though these were misdemeanor charges, the entire district attorney's office had eyes on this case. That was why they'd asked for a three-to-six-year sentence for Fats, a punishment well beyond the guidelines for a young man with no prior record.

The judge seemed to be learning a lot. It was apparent that he'd never had a meaningful conversation with someone who'd served time before. He began to question me directly.

"How would you describe solitary confinement?"

"Torture."

"How many correctional facilities have you been in?"

"Seven."

"Would you say that some were better than others?"

"No."

"So they were all the same?"

"Prison is prison. I would never describe one jail as being better than another; I could only describe different types of oppression."

I refused to break eye contact with the judge as he tried his best to corner me with his questions. It wasn't long before he realized his attempts to confuse and frustrate me weren't working.

It was time to deliberate.

After thanking me for my testimony, the judge excused himself and retreated to his chambers. I found my way back to my seat and waited anxiously for the sentence.

You could hear a pin drop.

Prayers trickled out from the crowd; Fats's mom began to cry, overwhelmed with the thought of her boy doing more time. You could feel the collective silently hoping. Wishing. Waiting. I'd never imagined that a sentencing for such low-level offenses would warrant that amount of time and energy, but when you're found not guilty for the murder of a police officer's son, the justice system works a little different.

After what felt like an eternity, the judge returned with his ruling. He had decided to sentence Fats to probation. Fats would finally be released after spending years in jail for a crime he didn't commit. The room burst into applause and cheers; he was coming home.

Now Fats works with the Youth Art & Self-Empowerment Project. He helps run the participatory defense hub offering support to young people and their families who've been impacted by the system. If someone were to ask me today if I know Fats personally, I'd be honored to say I do. He is no longer a young man behind enemy lines. He is a brother, a comrade, a leader in this movement. Now Fats goes to court to advocate for others. He's been actively organizing to end youth incarceration in Pennsylvania. He is also a community expert. We all are.

Montgomery County, Pennsylvania
Testify
Heather Lewis
NORRISTOWN HUB

I wasn't but two years into becoming a practitioner of participatory defense when my son Sabiir was charged with crimes that could have his young nineteen-year-old self serving twenty years in prison.

As a mother who spent nearly twenty years working in community service, I knew that I needed to be involved with his case and make sure that everything was done for him to get the best outcome. Thankfully, participatory defense gave me the tools to do so, despite my severe anxiety about my son's future. But just because I knew the steps to take didn't necessarily mean the system was just going to back down from incarcerating my son for more years than he had been alive.

I started with participatory defense in Montgomery County, Pennsylvania, in 2018. I was introduced to the model by Montgomery County's then chief public defender at the time, Keir Bradford-Grey. She had brought together over a hundred people who had all fought for the well-being of our community in various ways, to hear from families and organizers from California who had been using the approach for years. In the crowd was the late Herbert A. Morris, the fatherhood director of our service agency, who had a passion for helping men be better versions of themselves. He saw participatory defense as a key addition to his effort to support the many families we saw who had to pick up the pieces after an incarceration. We started having weekly meetings to make participatory defense a community reality for those of us who have seen policing and jails decimate our neighborhoods. Our service agencies were often there to help support after incarceration, to offer resources, reentry services, basic life necessities. But what if we intervened before the incarceration did its damage?

The challenge we faced was that participatory defense is not a service model and we were in a nonprofit service industry. We had to unlearn certain behaviors in order to effectively empower families rather than see them as "clients," especially those who were used to having services provided to them. Also, getting the public defenders on board with working with us was challenging, even though the head of that agency fully supported using participatory defense. And then, we needed to build trust within our own community so that, together, we could actually win back the freedoms that were being taking from us on a regular basis. Overcoming the guilt, shame, and embarrassment many feel when they find themselves involved in the criminal legal system took some time, even though we were directly impacted ourselves. But our meetings consistently grew, mainly through the participation of women of color.

As my son's case started, I developed a heightened sense of compassion for mothers, grandmothers, sisters, and aunties who come to our meetings supporting their husbands, sons, cousins, fathers, and brothers who are fighting criminal cases. It was clear based on the overwhelmingly female makeup of our meetings that the criminal legal system had a bead on our Black and Brown males. In ways that reminded me of conditions under slavery, husbands, sons, uncles, and fathers are ripped from their families for decades of incarceration, leaving Black and Brown women to hold their families together. We used our meetings not just to strategize on how to get our men back, but also to communally support one another as women navigating life without our loved ones. I am grateful that we have continued that work and remain a resource for other women, expediting the process of working through a case, collectively beginning the healing process from the trauma of a court case, and ensuring that our community members are not bounced around from service provider to service provider.

Montgomery County is one of the most affluent communities in Pennsylvania, with very few people of color in traditional leadership roles. The demographic makeup of Montgomery County as of July 2021 was 79 percent white, 10 percent Black, 8 percent Asian, and 6 percent Hispanic. The targeting of people of color by the system, in that context, is even starker. For our hub, we weren't just taking on individual cases but, in a larger sense, we were challenging the status quo and demanding that the voices of poor Black and Brown people be heard. Participatory defense is ultimately about our community's survival.

When my son got charged, I thought I was well positioned to help after two years of supporting other families in the same situation. I had the chief public defender's direct number, I had even trained many public defenders through our community organizing support work, but I still found it difficult to get basic answers to questions about my son's case from his assigned public defender. Fortunately, one of the foundational principles of participatory defense is empowerment—and sometimes that means pushing the public defenders to be responsive to the people they are representing.

After months of building trust, we made progress in understanding each other and how we would use participatory defense as a supplement to the public defender's advocacy. We were able to start working together as a team, and developed a plan to reduce the decades of incarceration Sabiir was facing. Knowing what to expect from each stage in the court process, and being able to communicate that to Sabiir, helped calm his anxiety, even though he was locked up while facing these charges. Knowing I was working with his attorney allowed him to more easily trust his public defender as well, which made it that much easier for his attorney to do her job and accomplish what we all wanted: Sabiir home as soon as possible.

But true to the system's nature to throw roadblocks in your way, Sabiir was assigned a new attorney! We essentially had weeks to get the new attorney up to speed on a year's worth of work. This was frustrating to Sabiir, but he trusted our process, and it turned out that his new attorney was very much in favor of participatory defense.

Ultimately, it all came down to an open plea hearing, where the judge would have full discretion to decide the length of Sabiir's sentence. Our focus was on how to impact what the judge understood about my teenage son sitting before him. He needed to know Sabiir—the challenges he faced growing up and his future outside of a prison cell. That was a family story, and it was for us to tell. We were the experts of our own lives.

Having two years under my belt as a participatory defense practitioner does not mean that I was an expert in every situation. The organic nature of the hub meant that we addressed situations and developed strategies as needed; we learned as we walked this road. Sabiir's upcoming hearing was the first time we needed to prepare a family—my family—to testify in court.

I wanted the court to know that my son was the only boy in a family of three sisters and a mother who he believed he had to protect. I wanted the court to know that his stepfather was abusive and that my son was young and felt helpless and began to lash out. He also experienced the trauma of gun violence at the age of seventeen. It was important for the prosecutor and judge to be aware of the trauma he experienced at such a young age.

His new attorney welcomed our presence in court and agreed that it was a good idea to have us testify on Sabiir's behalf. I prepared his grandmother and two sisters to speak about him and what he meant to them.

As my mother and I talked about getting on the stand and testifying to who her grandson was to her, her rising anxiety level prompted her to reveal her own experiences with PTSD, as a result of being a mother with two Brown sons in a predominantly white community. Waves of anxiety and stress washed over her as she remembered the violence and the police presence that peppered my childhood. It is an emotional journey to think about the oppressive and punishing role police and the system had played in our family across generations. Sabiir's young sisters were quite happy to speak on their brother's behalf and let him know just how much they loved him, how he was always looking out for them, how he was a present and attentive big brother. We all took the stand and shared our love for my son. I was not prepared for the emotion that poured out of me when it was my turn. My own guilt and shame and feelings of failure as a mother took over. Instinctively, I wanted to protect my son and absorb his pain. What a transformative moment for us all. The DA did not have any questions for us—I don't think there was anything for him to even ask. However, the judge was so moved by the testimony that he asked my son if he realized how loved he was. Probably until that moment, he had not.

What could have been a twenty-year sentence—meaning my son would be nearly forty years old upon his release—was reduced to a two-year sentence with the recommendation that he go to a youth offenders prison where he would have access to programs.

On September 19, 2019, I picked my son up from SCI Dallas, with his eleven-year-old sister in tow as a surprise, and we made the two-hour drive home where his sisters, grandparents, and participatory defense family greeted him with hugs, tears, and laughter.

My son has since held gainful employment, established a music career, and started a family of his own, giving me two grandsons. He uses music as therapy for himself and as a means of reaching other young men to share the knowledge that they have options beyond criminal activity as a means of supporting themselves or as an outlet for their trauma. He sits in on meetings here and there, offering guidance from his experience, and offers feedback on court watching.

I look forward to seeing what the next chapter of his life brings.

My son's victory was very personal and directly impacted every aspect of my life from his arrest until his release, and I am honored to walk that journey with other families as a guide, as a shoulder to cry on, and as another proud mama when their loved ones come home.

Part II
TYPES OF CASES

3

BAIL AND PRETRIAL DETENTION

Nothing shows the cold, callous, assembly-line efficiency of the court system more than arraignment hearings. They are the first court dates, when people hear what they are being charged with and learn whether they'll be able to fight their charges while outside or if they will have to take on the most significant challenge of their lives while incarcerated. Due to a predatory money bail system, it is also where a bail amount may be imposed, and when people have to make gut-wrenching decisions around how much they are willing to pay for their freedom.

For families in the courtroom pews waiting for their detained loved one's case to be called, it can be a chaotic frenzy that can be over before they know it started. It may be the first time since the arrest and detention that they have seen their loved one, in a colored jumpsuit, shackled or handcuffed, sitting in the box waiting for the case to be called. In Santa Clara County, when we first started attending arraignment courts more frequently, what stood out the most besides the outrageous bail amounts was how quickly people were "processed" in such an important stage in the court process. Judges seemed to make decisions at the pace of grocery store clerks—moving items, scanning them, bagging them. Typically, at arraignment court, there would be one public defender representing every person who had a case. Because they had usually just received the cases, the attorneys didn't have time to get to know the people they were representing enough to make a strong personalized case on their behalf. They might ask for bail to be lowered from the scheduled amount associated with a charge. The prosecutor might assert that the high bail amount was justified or might even ask for it to be raised. Then the judge would rule, usually in favor of the scheduled bail amount. The defendant usually couldn't afford the exorbitant bail and would be taken back to the jail; meanwhile, the court moved on to the next case. These devastating bail decisions would happen in less time than it takes for someone to drink a glass of water.

The families who attended our weekly participatory defense meetings usually had loved ones locked up pretrial, so they had already been through the arraignment hearing and were given a bail amount they couldn't afford. In California, the average bail amount is set at $50,000—far beyond the reach of most people. Consequently, California jails are overwhelmingly filled with people who have been detained pretrial, meaning they haven't actually been convicted of a crime. In Santa Clara County, on any given day, over 80 percent of our jail is filled with people being held pretrial. These numbers mirror the national landscape. Currently, over 400,000 people are estimated to be detained pretrial in jails across the country, making up 67 percent of all people in city and county jails.

When people are detained pretrial, they risk losing their jobs, homes, and family stability. Prosecutors know this, so it's no coincidence that people are more likely to plea while locked up—whether or not they're guilty of the crime they've been accused of—just to get out as soon as possible. Our plea rate in Santa Clara is aligned with the national numbers, which show that 97 percent of all criminal cases are resolved with plea deals. The relationship between astronomical pretrial detention rates and high plea rates is not coincidence, it's causal. People with high bail amounts can be detained for years pretrial. This means that the set bail amount is pivotal in determining what direction a case can take—whether leading straight to prison or back home. If you can get your bail amount reduced, or even better, get released without bail, you can avoid being in debt to a bail bonds company and feeling forced to take whatever plea deal the prosecutor offers. Without the sledge-hammer of pretrial detention, prosecutors have to rely on the merits of their cases alone, which usually means getting charges dropped or reduced.

Watching the high-speed incarceration machine grind through people at arraignment court, we realized that intervention early in the adjudication process could mean not only pretrial freedom, but also being in a much better position to fight and beat a case if charges were still being pursued by the DA's office. And the reality was, the people who held the potential to not only intervene but win freedom at the arraignment hearings were often sitting in the courtroom pews. They were the families and community members who the public defender could tap into to make the argument for release or a bail reduction. The two criteria on which judges were supposed to be making their bail decisions were the person's likelihood of returning to court and public safety. If the people in court who really knew the person's circumstances—including information on the consequences of detention, the support systems on the outside that could ensure the person made court dates, and information that could prove the case never should have been filed at all, or was being overcharged—could get that information to a defense attorney, it could transform that first court date.

But we realized that when an arrest happened, families didn't necessarily know how to locate their loved one in jail, how to find out when the court date was, or how to get information—sometimes time-sensitive information—to the defense attorney. This was true everywhere a participatory defense hub existed. It was common for us to get a frantic call in the middle of the night in which someone would say, "They just arrested her; what can I do?" We shared with families how to look up arraignment dates, and what information they should gather for the public defender to make an argument for release. If they knew anything about the alleged incident, we would ask them to memorialize that information by writing it down or recording it so the defense attorney could use it to challenge the case right away. In the lifetime of a court case, people's memories fade and potential witnesses helpful to the defense move. Sometimes, by the time the defense attorney wants to start investigating a case to mount a trial strategy, all that material is gone. So even if this case is going to be won or lost at trial at some point in the future, what happens within the very first days and hours after an arrest could determine whether or not that story ends with freedom.

Over the years, we got so used to these types of calls that we decided it could be effective if we shared the action steps more widely. We put it all on a poster and a handout we called "The First 24," or, what you can do within the first twenty-four hours of the arrest of a loved one. In some ways, it was an attempt to regain some measure of control in a moment of chaos and fear. And it had tangible impact. Families would head into arraignments with a plan, already linked up with the public defender, ready to secure a release and already gathering what they needed to beat the charge completely. Participatory defense hubs across the country created the First 24 for their respective counties, all templatized around the same basic questions that people would ask themselves after the arrest of a loved one. The First 24 was a tool used to fight back against a system that was designed to place people facing charges and their public defenders a lap behind prosecutors and police by the very first court date.

But even if people aren't able to get to the First 24, the overall urgency of acting early to impact pretrial detention and bail decisions has become paramount within participatory defense hubs. In fact, one of the first questions a family is asked when they walk into a participatory defense meeting is about the pretrial detention and bail status of their loved one. Preventing pretrial detention or avoiding or lowering a high bail could have a compounding impact on the case moving forward, just as the system would have a mounting advantage with every passing day someone is detained pretrial.

The following stories share how hubs and families are challenging pretrial incarceration and money bail for individuals and entire communities. And it's not just within those early, immediate hours after arrest. Sometimes it's before arraignment, during arraignment, or getting a bail hearing after the initial arraignment didn't go as hoped. An intervention could even take multiple bail hearings over a series of months. These critical court decisions have become too routinized toward detention, so part of the effort is changing how bail decisions are made entirely. Hubs are doing this by fighting for changes in bail law, or making sure courts honor the reforms that exist on paper but rarely get applied unless judges feel pressure from communities. Hubs might connect with community bail funds to get away from bail bond companies that have extracted money from communities of color for generations. These bail funds pay the full bond for the release, with no charge or fee to the person. Sometimes hubs gather specific information in advance of a quickly approaching court date so that the call for pretrial release can be an individualized community call for getting someone out of custody. The pieces in this section show the spectrum of what is being tried both as new models of pretrial justice and as examples of what has been done in those volatile, and often dark, moments of bail hearings. Though varied in approach and based on the respective realities and needs of different communities at different moments in time, there is a common dominator to the approach: acting together as early as possible. If the court system is a well-oiled, efficient, carceral machine, participatory defense can be the wrench in its gears, slowing it down and even stopping it.

Santa Clara, California
Winning My Dad's Pretrial Freedom
Natalie Gonzalez

ALBERT COBARRUBIAS JUSTICE PROJECT

It was a complete shock when my father was arrested for serious allegations. While I was going through my normal routine of working and taking care of the kids, I assumed he was also working and living his life. But he was actually being taken into custody, detained, and having his first court date, which I later learned is called an arraignment. I didn't attend that court hearing because I didn't even know he was in custody or that he had a first court date. I came to later find out that this is where they read him his charges and he was given a bail amount I didn't even know was possible—over one million dollars! It was clear they wanted to keep him locked up.

Once I found out he was in jail from my aunt (my dad's sister), I immediately tried looking him up online, but wasn't able to find anything because I had no clue where to start. I didn't know where he was being held, when his next court date was, or what if anything I could do to help. It turned out that my aunt met some people at my dad's court date who were part of a group that could support us as a family to get some answers about my dad. They were called De-Bug and had meetings every week with other families in the same shoes as we were. She started going to these meetings, and we would talk after about what she learned about how the court worked and what next steps we could take. She said we as a family needed to be at his next court date and gave us all the time and location. It seems small, but knowing I had at least a little bit of information to start working to get my dad out was a really big deal.

As we waited for the court date, my emotions were all over the place. I was so hurt that he had been inside all alone. I was scared that I might never get to hold or hug him again. Was he able to stay warm during the cold winter nights? Did he have anything edible to eat?

I attended his next court date not exactly knowing at the time what it was for or what to expect, but it turned out it was for him to be assigned a new attorney. The new attorney went up to my dad, spoke to him briefly, addressed the court, and my dad was given his next court date. I felt that not much was actually done, and everything happened so fast. I began heading out the doors of the courtroom thinking, "What am I going to do?!" Am I just going to sit in these courtrooms, see my dad handcuffed, then leave when he goes back behind the doors, headed back to the jail? But when we walked out of the courtroom, my aunt and a few of the De-Bug people began talking with my dad's new attorney. This was something I didn't even know we could do, and I was pretty shocked that she freely came up to talk to us. This was a super helpful step because his attorney was able to meet his support system, and we agreed to a future meeting with her in order to talk about my dad's bail. She was also able to explain to us what her plan was for my dad and how she was planning to submit a motion to reduce his bail and ask for a hearing. I was excited to hear this news, and a bit surprised. I always assumed that attorneys did not speak to family members about plans. This attorney was completely different because she was nice, listened to everything I had to say, and she was working with the whole family. She saw us as a team.

At the De-Bug meeting, we planned out how we as a family could impact what the attorney was going to submit in the motion to reduce bail. We met with the attorney about a few weeks later, and together came up with a release plan for my dad, addressing any concerns the judge might have. For pretrial release, the two main issues that were argued about were "safety" and whether he would come back to make his court dates if let out of custody. The attorney wanted us to provide a description of my dad's work, community support, housing, and finances. We were presenting all this information to convince the judge to consider my dad's limited ability to pay so they could give him an affordable bail. Now that we knew what specific information we needed to gather and put together for the attorney to make her argument, we as a family all worked on our assignments. We were putting together what they called at De-Bug a "social biography packet" that was targeted to reduce the bail amount so my dad could fight his charges on the outside. Over the course of these weeks, I attended the meetings at De-Bug so we could make sure we were all moving forward, and I was learning a lot about bail hearings. From what my aunt told me, when they first decided on my dad's bail at arraignment, the court was going through a bunch of people's cases, so they didn't devote much time to my dad; they just landed on a huge bail amount. At this upcoming bail hearing, my dad's case would be the only one being discussed, his attorney was going to be able to make a full argument, and we could share more details about who my dad was, and who stands with him.

The day of my dad's bail hearing came, and we arrived prepared with his release plan and all of his support. My dad's brothers, sister, nieces, nephews, and community were all there to support him. We packed the courtroom. I felt nervous but confident with the information we had gathered. The attorney was able to present the social biography packet that we put together, showing that my dad was going to be living away from the complaining witness, had a job he could come back to if released, and would continue being a coordinator and sponsoring people for his AA group. We also created a schedule of his weekly routine and we showed that he would have the support of all family members by making sure he made it back to every single one of his court dates. My dad's attorney walked the judge through all the information, and there wasn't much the DA could say in response. The judge was so impressed with everything that she agreed to release my dad on a $5,000 bond plus some conditions of release.

My dad was released that night and I was able to see him the very next day. It was the best feeling being able to see and hug him once again instead of seeing him through glass at jail visits. My dad and I became closer and created a stronger bond. He also started attending weekly participatory defense meetings and speaking about his experience to families going through the same thing. When they saw him at the meetings after being released from jail, knowing he started with an even higher bail amount than them, they knew that freedom was possible for their loved one too. We also got to work closer with his attorney, and he was able to be a part of strategy meetings in order to help his case rather than sitting inside jail waiting for his next court date.

After what my dad and family went through, and what we were able to accomplish, I wanted to support other families who were in the same shoes I was in. I now am one of the De-Bug organizers that a family connects with at arraignment court. I am the person my aunt connected with at my dad's arraignment years ago. I try to remember that time when I meet a new family at court—the feeling of not knowing even what questions to ask, but wanting to do whatever you can while seeing your loved one in shackles waiting for their name to be called. When I sit with them in the back of the court, or in the hallway, and explain the bail process, I tell them about my experience. Then they start sharing more about their loved ones' lives, what is waiting for them at home, and why it is so important for them to be free. I tell them I understand— that I've been there, and that even though it looks dark right now, freedom is possible and their support can mean everything to make that happen.

Durham, North Carolina
Court Mobbin' in Bull City
Andréa "Muffin" Hudson
BULL CITY PARTICIPATORY DEFENSE HUB

Sixty-one. That was the number of days I was incarcerated in 2013. I started counting my days when the person sharing that cell with me was leaving, and on the day that she left, I realized I had been there for thirty days.

By the sixtieth day I couldn't take it anymore. I asked one of the women in jail with me to call her friend to call my friend and ask them to sell my Ford Explorer to get me out. Enough was enough. I missed my kids, and I really thought that a shooting that I saw on the news was my kids. It said a young girl driving an SUV with a young black male were shot at a stoplight and the young man didn't survive. I couldn't get information about what color the SUV was, and I was slowly losing my mind. I kept thinking about my children. I knew they were out in the world without their mom, and no one—and I do mean no one—would care about or love them like me. My daughter was only seventeen years old at the time and took care of her seven-year-old little brother. Even now, I think about the harm and trauma that they live with because we were separated during my incarceration.

When I was released from jail, I was embarrassed and ashamed. I kept thinking: my mom didn't raise me to go to jail even though I knew I wasn't guilty. I felt people would judge me and look down on me, and I didn't want that. I didn't want the stigma that went along with incarceration. I pled guilty to something that I didn't do because I wanted to get out and go home.

Getting arrested and sitting in jail was a very pivotal moment in my life. Before my arrest I was in school for criminal justice and I wanted to be a probation or parole officer, but going to jail made me realize that I didn't want to be an overseer nor would I want to be a dictator, so I dropped out of school and started to look for work full time. I finally found an agency that would hire me with the charges on my background, and in doing that, my supervisor advised me that instead of making $15 per hour it would be $9.75 per hour because she was taking a chance on hiring me. I became a private duty nurse.

One day, I saw a Facebook Live with Umar "Salute" Muhammad, a founding member of All of Us or None Durham, a grassroots civil and human rights organization fighting for the rights of formerly—and currently—incarcerated people and their families. He was promoting a "Clean Slate" clinic where you could learn how to get your criminal record expunged. I went even though I thought it was a fraud. I am from New York, and the police there used to do this thing where they would send letters saying people had won tickets to a game or won a TV but then arrest them because of outstanding warrants. I feared this would happen to me if I attended the clinic. But I was tired of my charges holding me back, so I went anyway. I'm glad I did because it wasn't a fraud. Far from it.

At the expungement clinic, I talked to an attorney about my

charges and was told they would file the paperwork for me to get my expungement. Six months later I got my expungement paperwork, so I wanted to be effective and pay it forward like Umar encouraged us to. I joined All of Us or None, and that's when I learned about training being offered on "participatory defense." SpiritHouse, a partner of All of Us or None, invited us to the training. Three people from an organization called Silicon Valley De-Bug came. As I was going through the training, I was thinking, "This is amazing and I have been doing this work but didn't have a name for it and now I do: it's participatory defense." It lit a fire in me that I knew was burning and gave a name and community to what I had been doing intuitively.

The model was put to the test in the middle of training when Brian was arrested. I had known Brian previously; Umar introduced us at the Clean Slate clinic. He had finished one year of being out of prison after being tried as an adult when he was a youth and subsequently incarcerated. Brian attended the first two days of the participatory defense training but didn't show up on the third day. He called me that morning and said he was on his way, but then was getting ready to go back to his house because the police had called him and said that they were going to arrest his mother if he didn't come back to his house. His mother was disabled. It was their first time living together after he spent all those years in prison. He was proud to be able to take care of her. They had just moved in to that house two days prior.

I was trying to get him to wait for us so we could be there with him, but he said, "No, I'm going now," and to just meet him at the jail. That's when I told everybody in the training that Brian had gotten arrested and was headed to jail. Even though our De-Bug folks had another half-day planned for the training, we all decided there was no better time to start doing participatory defense than with Brian, right then and there. All I could think of was that

Brian was my friend, my little brother, and I wanted to try everything and anything to get him out.

I got the marker and got in front of the whiteboard. I put his name on the board—Brian—and he became our first case. We started with updates, so we all knew what was happening, and then we talked about what we needed to do—our next steps. We knew we had a timeline. We knew Brian was turning himself in at his house, and it was going to take some time for them to take him to the jail. So we thought about who we needed to call and why: the jail to see about bail, the district attorney to see about charges, the jail for his specific location. We found out through the jail that his bond was $500,000 and that's when we were like, Oh . . . he's staying there overnight. That's a pretty high bond, and we didn't have that kind of money. We talked to a bail bondsman who said that he would help us but we had to have 10 percent, and that's when Umar and I started calling people for money to try to make the 10 percent. But we couldn't come up with $50,000.

We thought maybe we could try to get a bond reduction by showing up at court the next morning for Brian's first appearance—some of the specific steps we had just discussed in the participatory defense training. And everyone was, like, yeah, let's do it. We thought about who could show up for him—so that was us, his friends, All of Us or None, SpiritHouse, and his girlfriend at the time. The De-Bug folks wrote a letter for him, even though they had just met him two days before that. But Brian really struck everyone at that training. He can be a quiet guy, but he spoke up a lot at the participatory defense training. We also talked to his mom. This was difficult for her because she had been down this road before, and she sure didn't want to go through it again. She had medical issues, had no transportation, and Brian was her caregiver. So it was hard for her to come to court. I volunteered to call her and help her write a letter about how Brian took care of her, paid her bills, took care of his daughter, and how she was really looking forward to living together after incarceration had separated them for years.

The next morning, we all showed up at court. The bottom floor of the jail is where they hold first appearances. Here in Durham County, if you're arrested, you usually see the magistrate, and if you don't make bail, you'll see a judge the next morning unless it's the weekend, or holidays. That day, about thirteen of us showed up for Brian. While waiting for court to start, we talked about who was going to speak and what to highlight. We all said let's all speak and tell the judge how much Brian means to us and how we would support him. There are only four rows in appearance court, and we took up three of them. That's what I called "court mobbin'," a practice that we still use years later as a hub.

The door connecting the jail to the court opened, and we saw Brian shackled to other people—about eight to ten—and walking in a single line. They were ordered to walk past a big glass window and not to look at the audience, which was us, on the other side. I thought that was so cruel because people just want to see if their loved ones are in the crowd of faces, even if it's on the other side. They were then told to sit on a very long bench. Once they were all seated, it moved pretty quickly. There was one public defender who spoke to everyone and was speaking for everyone. We saw him talk to Brian.

As we sat and watched them bring people in and out that courtroom, I couldn't help but compare this to a modern-day auction block where people are given unrealistic bond amounts that will ensure that they are held captive. They were all Black and Brown faces. I looked at them as hostages of a cruel system.

We sat there waiting for Brian's turn. There was a young man before Brian was called who faced similar charges to him, some involving drugs. He had a $500,000 bail like Brian. The judge said that bond wasn't high enough and doubled it.

My heart sank a bit. We started whispering to each other, because we weren't supposed to talk to each other in court. And we were, like, there was no way Brian was getting out now! We couldn't even come up with $50,000. If this judge doubled Brian's bond, how were we supposed to come up with $100,000? He was going to be stuck. And what would that do to Brian's mental state—making it through his first year of being out of incarceration, and then facing it again?

When they escorted the young man out, they called Brian's name. The judge was asking him questions that we couldn't really hear. And the judge looked out in the gallery and asked if there was anyone out there for this person? All three rows of us stood up and started forming a line by the microphone that was on the side of the wall by the big glass. (By the way, if we hadn't gone to court the day before, we wouldn't have even known there was a microphone on that side.)

The judge looked at all of us and said something like, "Oh no no no—you guys can pick one person and the rest of you guys can sit down." At first we were a little hesitant, but if this judge doubled the bail of the young man right before Brian without any prodding, there was no telling what he could do with Brian.

So, we picked Nia Wilson from SpiritHouse to speak—and she did. She explained that Brian had a job at SpiritHouse, that he was the main caregiver for his disabled mother and his daughter, and asked for his bond to be reduced dramatically so we could possibly get him out and he could get home to his mom. When Nia sat down, the judge read over the papers and letters on his dais, and said, "Okay, your bond is $500,000. I will reduce it to $50,000 and that's as low as I will go.

Umar and I turned to each other and said, "Okay, we gotta come up with some money now so we can try to get Brian home" that night. We talked to a bail bondsman who said if we could give him $500, then he would be okay with some kind of monthly payment plan that would add up to the 10 percent and he would get Brian out ASAP.

That night, we were able to get Brian home. He was inside, of course, so he didn't know everything that we were doing outside to get him out, but once he was out, we told him about the arrangement of the bail and he said he would take over the payments from there. That's when I knew participatory defense worked—we turned that judge, and if we could convince that judge, we knew we could convince others. Brian went home and got on his social media and told all his friends about participatory defense and how we brought him home. That's how our circle started to grow: he had friends and family who were facing charges, and they would call me and say they needed support.

After Brian got home, we kept working with him. He got his police report from his attorney, and we read it together to point out any discrepancies, and identified where the case against him was based on lies. We also kept building his social biography packet. While he was out fighting the charges, he was able to keep his job, continue to be involved in the community, and, most important, he was able to take care of his mom and daughter and pay their rent. The charges ultimately got dismissed, and that was a big win for Brian and for all of us.

But that's when the problem of bail became really disturbing for me. When his charges were dismissed, we went back to the bail bondsman to tell him. We had no idea that Brian had to keep paying the payments even though he was done with his case. So even though it was a victory, he still had to keep paying for his freedom. A few months later, Brian got arrested again. By that time, I had started to research North Carolina's bail laws, and found out that when someone is arrested, a magistrate is supposed to consider making a bond unsecure first—meaning seeing if they can just release someone with a promise to appear in court.

So, when he called me after he was arrested, another organizer, Tia, and I went to the magistrate, and I thought, Why don't we try asking if they will make his bond an unsecure bond? At that time, his bond was $15,000. I told the magistrate that Brian couldn't afford to pay anything, and he was already paying a debt to a bondsman for a case in which the charges were dismissed. The magistrate said that he didn't think he could because the charges required an automatic forty-eight-hour hold. I pushed back on the logic of the hold. The magistrate said he would look into it. The magistrate came out after a while and told us that he was going to make his bond unsecure because he had faith that we were going to ensure Brian would come to court. His bond was really high and it would look strange if he were not in court. They (the lawyers, the judge) could come back to me and say, Why would you unsecure this man's bond and he doesn't show up at court. I said, "Trust me. He's showing up at court to take care of this." The next day, Brian did go to court. He actually beat me to court. He called me from the courthouse and said, "Where you at?" He said, "I wanted to make sure YOU were still coming."

A couple of months later, Brian was killed. He was shot multiple times in the parking lot of his home. It was a really heartbreaking time for his family and for us. I remember being at court for someone else when the clerk called Brian's name out. It was his court date for the charge he had. That's when I broke down, hearing his name said in court. I told the court Brian was dead, and I didn't understand why his name was still on the docket. They said the court had no way to update the system with news of someone's death. It made me think that when Brian died, he died with all that debt that he still owed to the system.

I didn't think it was fair for people to have to pay a bondsman even if their court case is dismissed simply because they made a payment arrangement. I started to have conversations with people who were doing local organizing around the unjust bail system. That led to us starting the North Carolina Community Bail Fund of Durham so that people who couldn't afford bail didn't have to sit in jail while waiting for their cases to be resolved, and when they were done with it, they didn't have to owe anyone. They were just free. We have bailed out hundreds of people here in Durham, and in every county in North Carolina. Bail in our state can start on average at about $3,000 but can run anywhere from $1,000 to $1,000,000. Most people face housing challenges, and their charges stem from just trying to survive and keep their heads above water. We usually get a list of people every morning who are incarcerated in jail. We go to first appearance court for them where we ask the judge to unsecure the bond first—especially when there is family and/or us as community who can help the person go to court. If the judge doesn't unsecure it and the bond is low, then the Community Bail Fund goes and pays the bond. We have folks fill out an intake form that asks them about their needs, their contact number and name of a family or friend who can act as their emergency contact number, and their case information (next court date, charges, attorney if they know it). When we are able to bail people out, we also offer them the chance to join participatory defense meetings so that we can further support them in their cases. Most people end up joining the meetings.

But when the bail is really high and we can't bail them out, we encourage their families to come to a participatory defense meeting where we can help them create a social biography packet, work with their attorneys, and help push for a bond hearing where there is a chance for the bond to be reduced or unsecured then.

I don't do the bail fund work without doing the participatory defense work. It's important that these two strategies to freedom run parallel, and one is not a condition of the other. When people say they need court support, I encourage them to come to the participatory defense meetings because that's how they will meet the people who will support them in court. That's where they'll meet the people who have gone through what they've gone through and get the help to navigate them through their case.

I've realized that when we bail people out it's not just about paying money to buy back their freedom but it is also an opportunity to help bail them out of life situations that lead them to incarceration. A lot of times, it's helping people find housing or helping with groceries. Sometimes, it's helping people reconcile and squashing their beef with people in the community. We don't need the system to criminalize or referee our communities.

From the time I sat in the jail facing my own charges, to the experience with Brian, and then now seeing what hundreds of people go through every day facing charges and feeling trapped—all of these experiences led me to this work that is really about freeing people. The web of the money bail structure is designed to trap us, even in death, like in Brian's situation. But like any structure, it can be torn down.

Santa Clara, California
Proving Innocence
Ramon Vasquez and Raj Jayadev
ALBERT COBARRUBIAS JUSTICE PROJECT

Ramon, a twenty-eight-year-old truck driver and father of two, was arrested and charged with murder with gang enhancements. He went from finishing a normal day at work to being handcuffed by a violent gang enforcement police unit, and booked into the Santa Clara County jail.

Ramon was not at the scene of the alleged incident, but nonetheless was picked up at gunpoint based on what the detectives considered "a matching description." The investigation described an "average sized Hispanic male" in his twenties with a tattoo on his neck who drove a nondescript beige sedan. Ramon was completely innocent of the charges.

Although Ramon felt confident in his public defender, his first attorney was replaced by another who left much to be desired. Despite facing a life sentence for a crime he did not commit, his new court-appointed attorney told him to just take a plea early on in his pretrial detention.

Ramon's wife Yvonne went to high school with a De-Bug member, had heard a bit about what families were doing at our center, and started coming to our participatory defense meetings for support. She was naturally in a state of shock, and at that point, we hadn't seen anything like Ramon's situation before.

He was a couple of months into his case by the time Yvonne came to De-Bug. Although he was detained the whole time, he and his family had no real sense of what, if anything, his attorney was doing for his defense.

So, Ramon's family began by trying to assess his attorney's

willingness to invest time and effort into the case. They emailed the attorney asking whether there had been an investigation or fact-finding effort on Ramon's behalf, which witnesses had been interviewed, how much he had delved into discovery materials (the evidence used in the case), and what his next steps would be. They also emphasized what the family already knew about the case: details of how Ramon was picked up, what happened when police confiscated items from his home, and proof of Ramon's whereabouts at the time of the incident. Ramon consistently called his attorney to request that he meet with his family. Eventually, the calls and emails worked. The family was able to arrange a series of meeting to create a timeline and plan of action for the attorney and investigator. Significantly, this meant that the family could follow up as needed to ensure that each and every step was taken.

The family also received a copy of the discovery. On a weekly basis, they spent hours scouring the materials together, comparing notes and observations. They found contradictory statements by police and witnesses, glaring holes in the investigation, and identified how the evidence actually pointed to Ramon's innocence rather than guilt. This was the first time we had rigorously dissected an investigation like this as a form of participatory defense. The more we dug, the more we were in disbelief that Ramon was arrested at all and infuriated that he was still locked up.

But the secondary question was how to communicate what we found and to whom. We were used to holding press conferences and rallies to publicize the truths of the injustice system. However, this demanded a more focused approach through which we could prove Ramon's innocence during the court deliberation process itself. We needed his attorney to fully grasp the evidence of his innocence and to use it immediately.

Ramon's family collated their research and analysis into a document they titled "Ten Evidence-Based Reasons That Prove Ramon's Innocence." The list also included a request from Ramon and the family to conduct a polygraph test. Though not admissible in court, a passed polygraph test can be cited by an attorney while negotiating with the prosecutor. In some ways, Ramon and his family also wanted another way to ensure his attorney's buy in. Fortunately, the attorney ordered the polygraph. Ramon passed—twice.

The lawyer then met with the prosecutor and presented his evidence, including the findings of the family and community, plus the two passed polygraphs. Shortly after that meeting and six months after Ramon's arrest, the prosecutor agreed to drop the charges "due to insufficiency of the evidence." Ramon was released from his pretrial detention.

Once home, Ramon and his family were still determined to formally prove his innocence (rather than simply settling for the charges being dismissed). He asked his attorney to file a request for a "factual finding of innocence"—a finding that clears a person's name and record by affirmatively stating that they were innocent all along, but which is very rarely granted. However, Ramon was granted the factual finding of innocence, and, remarkably, his attorney said it was the first time in twenty-five years that he had been a part of one that had won. Unfortunately, Ramon had been fired from his job as a delivery driver when he was arrested and had to fight with management to get it back. But he ultimately succeeded, and is now a regional manager.

Santa Clara, California
The Day I Was Arrested and the Day I Was Released
Ramon Vasquez
ALBERT COBARRUBIAS JUSTICE PROJECT

When I Went In

Back in 2008, I was accused of murder in San Jose, California. I would never think this could or would happen to me, but life happens. It was a regular day at work until I got ready to go home. The nightmare began in the parking lot of my work as I walked to my car. I was swarmed by officers from a special unit of the San Jose Police Department.

As I was brought down to the homicide unit, I had no idea what was going on. I kept asking, "Why am I being arrested?" All my questions went unanswered and were met with shortness. Once at the station, I was questioned for hours by two homicide detectives playing good cop, bad cop with me over and over. Halfway through the interrogation, my senses told me to watch what I say because I figured out that these detectives were not interested in my story. Sitting in that cold room and knowing I was innocent, I had a battle with myself on whether I should ask for a lawyer or just explain my whereabouts so I could go home. Regrettably, I chose to keep talking so I could reason with these detectives and go home to my family. Looking back, what I learned from this was that if I thought I had information to prove my alibi, I shouldn't have told the detectives. The reason I say this is because I told them the apartment complex had a camera that oversaw my carport and you can see my car never left at the time of this crime.

What did I find out later? The detectives went to my apartment complex's management office, and the manager showed them the video. They saw that my car never left and took the hard drive, which was never to be found again.

Once I was sent to jail after the hours of questioning, I was scared that I made the wrong decision speaking to them. I was finally able to talk to my wife over the phone, and she said that she was being treated similarly to me. She told me, "We are not talking to them, they are not trying to help you!" I knew then that I was being falsely accused, and the police were going all in—not to figure out who committed the crime, but to convict me.

I was placed in forty-seven-hour lockdown, so I had a ton of time to reflect and strategize. Because of the charge, I was deemed ineligible for bail, but even if they assigned a bail amount, it would be beyond my reach. The first week in jail was a whirlwind and went by like a dream. The detectives said I had a "soft alibi" so I knew we needed more evidence. I found myself talking to my wife every other day. Those calls were all I had. I was completely blind to the outside world. On one of the calls, the first thing she said was, "Don't say nothing over the phone and we are getting support from a group." This made me even more curious about what was going on. I mean, she didn't even tell me the name of the organization, when they met, or what was going on. She found out from the organization that jail calls are recorded, so you could only communicate so much. But I felt better that she wasn't out there fighting for me alone.

I then immersed myself into my discovery packet to punch holes through their "Statement of Facts." I would spend hours on these study sessions, and would mail my "homework" to my wife weekly. She and my family and supporters from De-Bug would add what I found to their own readings of the discovery. This team approach was a godsend. It gave us hope and a plan of action.

As the months went by, though, I was getting very frustrated and impatient. I felt that actions without results were pointless, and I wasn't hearing much from my attorney. We would have court hearings, nothing would happen, and I would get yet another new court date. My wife could sense my despair, and in a call a day before another nameless court date, she said, "When you go to court, look into the crowd and see all the people with us." I made it a point to do just that during my next court date. I noticed that there were a lot of people sitting next to my family, all making eye contact with me, and sending me positive messages with their facial expressions.

One of those faces in the audience, Raj from De-Bug, visited me in jail that week, and we connected immediately. It felt like we knew each other long before this situation introduced us. We talked through our collective next steps. I always felt like my court-appointed attorney did no more than the bare minimum for me, but De-Bug and my family's persistence kept him accountable. The key for me on the inside was to never lose hope, to never become what they said I was, to be diligent about what I had started, and to have faith in the power of people.

When I Got Out

It was a Tuesday morning around eleven a.m. I was lying on my bunk bed, cold as always, thinking about the days to come. I was in a daze, deep in thought, when suddenly, the correctional officer came to my cell door and unlocked it. "Ramon, get up and get ready. You have court!" I told him it couldn't be me; I had had court yesterday and I would have court again on Thursday. He looked at me like I was stupid and said, "I don't know. They just called for you, so let's go."

I was led through the hallway to the elevator, then on to a holding cell. I was placed with some other guys who were going to court as well. We were all talking, and one of the guys asked me,

"What do you have today?" I replied, "I don't know. I'm not supposed to have court until Thursday." Then some scruffy man in the back said, "It's bad news, it's more charges!" After I heard that, my heart just stopped.

The sheriff came to the holding cell and called out, "Ramon, let's go!" I was placed in another elevator, then guided to yet another holding cell, this time by myself. As I sat there, I was shaking and my mind was racing.

My attorney entered a room that connected to my holding cell—he was on one side and I was on the other of the graffitied window. He took one look at me and said, "Don't look so sad. Didn't I tell you I would take care of you?" Then he just walked out. At that time the sheriff, an older lady, unlocked my cell door and led me inside the courtroom. When I walked into the courtroom, I looked to the right and I saw my friends and family, some crying, some smiling.

We all stood up as the judge came in and the hair on the back of my neck stood up too. The district attorney read off all the charges against me, and concluded, "We the people drop all the charges due to lack of evidence."

As I heard that, I dropped my head down with relief and finally let my guard down for the first time in five long months. The nightmare was over. I started crying and looked directly at the judge, who smiled back. As I was being removed from my seat, I looked at the DA and said "Thank you." He just said, "Yeah, I bet." I was then led to my holding cell and the sheriff said, "You can smile now, you're going home." That's when it really hit me. I fell to my knees in tears and thanked God for this miracle. I was led back to my floor and eventually to my cell. The hour I would be released could not have come any slower.

When I was finally released at about three in the morning, the first person I saw was my brother. He walked up and gave me the tightest bear hug I've ever felt. I was eager to see my wife, the woman who fought so hard for my innocence. She jumped out of the car and gave me a loving hug that was straight from her heart. That's when I knew my freedom was real, and I looked up at the jail in disgust.

4

YOUTH CASES

Every juvenile court we've walked into has the same aesthetic: some sort of fusion of a middle school classroom and a youth center, with eighties-style posters of encouragement on the wall, like a guy climbing a mountain and the word "perseverance" under it. On the tables are books for teens, inspirational biographies of historic figures like Martin Luther King Jr., Cesar Chavez, and Gandhi.

If you were sitting there alone, you might think that this is where a young person is supported, nurtured, and developed. But when the bailiffs, probation officers, prosecutors, and judges start their shifts and get to work, these interior designs contrast starkly with what happens to youth in this space.

On any given day, nearly sixty thousand youth under the age of eighteen are incarcerated in juvenile jails and prisons. The attempt to distance the juvenile legal system from the adult one is seen not only in the decoration of the rooms; it's in the language, their declared purpose. Juvenile court is supposed to be less expressly punitive and more about rehabilitation and development. The courts don't like to use the word "conviction" for youth; they use "adjudicated" instead. But the process is the same. The same abuses, assaults, and life-scarring harms that happen in adult prisons and jails happen in the juvenile prisons and jails—to kids.

When parents or older siblings come to participatory defense meetings for a young person, the energy in the room changes, becoming both more somber and more urgent at the same time. Participatory defense is an instinct to protect loved ones from the system. But with kids, that impulse to protect, to bring back, to make safe, taps into a deeper well.

Most of the youth our hubs have advocated for are facing the possibility of being charged as an adult, either through the discretion of the prosecutor or by the court. The stakes are so frighteningly high; it can mean a child facing years, decades, or life in prison. We know youth who faced these prospects before they could legally drive, or had been on a high school campus. Some were still playing Little League. The fierceness of parents, the deep ferocity to fight for their children, calls them to marshal any and all forces that will support their fight for their kids. They enter the room differently when they come to meetings, and the community responds differently too. Any family fight for a child is a battle for the life that hasn't been lived yet.

The decision to send a youth to adult court sounds bureaucratic and matter-of-fact, but it is perhaps the most morally audacious claim court actors make in the entire system. While the court language may have different terms based on jurisdiction, at its base the decision is a declaration that a young person is so irredeemable, so incapable of growth and change, that the right to a future must be taken away.

In this chapter, authors will share what these struggles have been like in different settings and situations, and how the experience shaped them. Our movement has had the incredible honor of being able to witness the lives that they fought for and the futures they extracted from the vise grips of the system. Our hubs get to go to the birthday parties, the graduations, the baby showers that the carceral system intended to erase from existence. Each milestone is a tribute to the triumph.

Just recently, our San Jose hub got to celebrate the seventieth birthday of our participatory defense matriarch, Gail Noble. The party was filled with family and friends, elders and babies, and every generation in between, sharing life updates, amazed at how people have grown or changed over the years that have passed since the last gathering. The man sitting next to Gail at her VIP table was her youngest son Karim, now in his early thirties—just like everyone here, dressed for the regal occasion. Gail watched him move around the room, beaming with pride.

We were sitting with Gail in juvenile court the first time we met Karim. He was fifteen years old, dressed in juvenile hall clothes, walking in with his head down. She was the first mom we knew that brought the community into juvenile court—the first mom we knew who stood up in court, without being asked or given permission, to demand freedom for her child. Her strength, and her invitation to the community to join her, was so bold and so insistent that the court would always save Karim's case until the end of the day, and for some inexplicable reason would have extra bailiffs in the court.

Gail would not relent, and got stronger with each hearing. And as a result, Karim did too. In juvenile hall visits, he would say how even the guards knew to treat him right, because none of them wanted Gail's energy focused on them. After several months, Gail won Karim's freedom. Her victory showed us all what the path to freedom would require and what it could result in. Years later, at this party, Karim became who his mom always knew he could be, living the life the system tried to take from him, from them. They have the same smile, Gail and Karim, and his kids will too.

This fight for youth justice is contained within such momentary time frames and individual cases. But its meaning and its implications span lifetimes and generations.

Santa Clara, California
Freeing Joseph from Adult Time
Gail Noble
ALBERT COBARRUBIAS JUSTICE PROJECT

I met Carol when her daughter and my son started dating a little after high school. She was kind, really watchful of her kids, and wanted the best out of them and for them. We got along from the moment we met.

One day she called me in a panic. Her younger son Joseph was picked up by police at school and arrested. She didn't know what to do. Police—SWAT—also came to her house and tore the place up and down. She had just gotten out of the shower, and when the police came, she put on some clothes really fast; they then made her and the rest of the family stand outside. She didn't know what to do. She and her husband Greg were devastated. I told them they should try to go to the jail to see Joseph, but they were caught between waiting for an attorney, a friend of a friend, to meet them at the house and going to see Joseph. They just kept waiting for this attorney to call them. They were just lost, and sad.

Joseph was only sixteen at the time. He was an athlete—he played basketball and was really good at it. He made varsity as a sophomore. Carol would make food for homeless people and go to the encampments, taking Joseph with her, and pass out food. When Carol got sick, Joseph kept doing the visits. He'd make food and take the plates over. He got his friends at the high school to help, and they would make the dinners, collect clothes, and pass them out themselves.

That's why when Carol and Greg found out what his charges were, they were just distraught. The Joseph they raised was a soft-spoken young man who cared about his family, loved football and basketball. But growing up as one of the only Black youth in his school and neighborhood, he often carried a certain kind of pressure alone. All of a sudden, Joseph found himself facing a slew of robbery charges and staring at a forty-plus-year sentence. Joseph was direct filed, meaning the district attorney immediately prosecuted him as an adult.

They had hired a private attorney to represent Joseph. I told them to come to De-Bug and they'd have the support of our organization. And I was so happy when they came. I was so proud to show them De-Bug, my second home, my family. I met De-Bug when my youngest son was arrested. I felt so alone, so unheard, until I met the folks at De-Bug. And the more I stayed and got involved, the more I felt myself getting stronger and my voice getting stronger. I had always been part of a movement. In high school in the late sixties, I helped lead sit-ins at my high school in East Palo Alto to demand that we learn about Black history from Black teachers. Being part of De-Bug awakens those feelings in me—of being bold, powerful, and fearless. People see De-Bug and they see a group of people who truly practice justice, and that scares them.

I wanted Carol and Greg to feel that too. At that meeting, we all sat around the red table with other families, talked about Joe's case, and came up with a list of questions they could ask the attorney so they could keep track of the representation that Joe needed. We knew some of these questions because there were other families too at De-Bug whose children were being tried as adults, same as Joe. One of them was a young boy, facing a life sentence at age fourteen. Even though his mom spoke Spanish and Carol and Greg spoke English, they understood each other's experiences.

One of the first things we did was create the social biography packet. They brought all their family pictures, and that process really helped them bring back a lot of memories of their family being together, all the barbecues and parties, and we spent time going over those pictures and listening to them tell the stories. It's a bittersweet process, because you're going through these photos, walking back through the memories, while your baby is alone, sitting in juvenile hall and facing more than forty years of prison away from you. You don't know what the outcome will be. And that's a scary, powerless feeling. But then at that same moment, you realize you're among people who are your support system, who are there to sit down with you and listen to all those stories, and be with you to challenge that fear.

It took us a while to put together the social biography packet, but Carol and Greg brought it proudly when we met with Joe's attorney for the first time. We had a list of questions and concerns in hand. Why hasn't he been making court appearances for Joe? Has he looked through the police reports and alleged "confession"? Had he gotten an investigator? What kind of investigation had he done on Joe's case?

He wasn't prepared for our questions. What shocked me the most was his response to our question about getting an investigator. He said he didn't say anything to Carol and Greg about hiring an investigator because he didn't think they could afford one. That meant that he hadn't done any investigation at all. I was so angry. Carol and Greg weren't even given a chance to decide whether or not to hire an investigator because the attorney thought they were too poor. Meanwhile, all this time had passed with Joe sitting in juvenile hall.

That's when the family decided to go with the public defender's office, and Joe ended up being represented by a fantastic, dedicated attorney in Mairead O'Keefe, who was thorough, communicative, and thoughtful. From the first meeting with her, it really felt like there was someone in Joe's corner sitting next to him in that box.

At the same time that we were building the social biography packet, gathering records, and getting witnesses to talk to the defense investigator, we at De-Bug had joined other organizations around California about this practice of DAs direct filing young people into the adult system and how to end it. We had a meeting at De-Bug with families and talked about collecting signatures for the initiative that we were hoping to get on the ballot that would stop this practice, as well as allow individuals to earn earlier parole dates once they had served their base terms. Carol, Greg, and I were at the meeting because we knew this could directly help Joe. We all signed up for different community events to collect signatures, and went to different churches and organizations. We would stand outside juvenile hall and talk to families. When I would go to these events and speak, I spoke of Joe's story. I had him on my mind.

The initiative, Proposition 57, got on the ballot in January 2016. And we went full force. Now the efforts were to push for voter turnout to pass that bill. Carol, Greg, and I and many De-Bug families would go out almost every weekend to encourage people to vote. Our families' lives were at stake. It was such a powerful time in De-Bug's history. We would fill buses and go up to Sacramento with all these families, coming together for Prop. 57. Families would drive three hundred miles from Southern California just for that meeting and we'd all support one another. And Prop. 57 gave us this way to align. I felt the stars align—for all our youth, especially Joe.

The night Prop. 57 passed, the first phone call we made was to Greg. We all teared up that night.

The next part of the battle was Joe's transfer hearing. Even though he could no longer be automatically tried as an adult because of Prop. 57, Joe still faced a transfer hearing in which a juvenile judge would decide whether he should stay in the juvenile system or be tried as an adult. We knew this was going to be an important hearing not just for Joe but also for a lot of youth in the system because it could set a tone for the rest of them. Joe's public defender hired a psychiatrist who evaluated Joe, and, listening to him, he really talked about how the neighborhood that Joe grew up in here in San Jose had been such a big influence. As parents, we don't really think of what kind of war zone our kids are stepping into when they leave the house, and how sometimes their lives are in danger.

Talking to that psychiatrist and then listening to him testify at the transfer hearing, Greg and Carol really got to thinking about moving their entire family to Fresno. They had originally lived there with the older kids, but then moved to San Jose to help take care of their parents. With Joe's situation, they thought about moving back again, especially because if Joe stayed in the youth system, the facility would be over there and they could see him all the time. They also wanted to show the court they were willing to do whatever it took to keep Joe safe. And that was a drastic decision for them, because their whole world was going to shift, but they made it anyway.

We helped Greg and Carol make a social bio video that really focused on that—the new house they were moving into, the decision they had made, and the new life they were re-creating, Joe's new future. It was a leap of faith. And already, Joe himself was making great strides inside juvenile hall. He graduated from high school, which his family got him to attend inside, completed a lot of programs, and was supported by the counselors. He sought his own counseling to address past traumas, and became a role model for other youth inside.

With the new transfer hearing laws, the probation officer gets to make a recommendation on whether to keep someone in the juvenile system or to try the youth in adult court. In Joe's case, the probation officer recommended that he stay in the youth system.

Despite the district attorney opposing Joe remaining in the juvenile system, the judge agreed that Joe should stay, and recognized Joe's growth and especially the different circumstances he would be coming home to. Greg, Carol, and Joe were so grateful, and it was a big release for them, as if they had been holding their breath this whole time.

At De-Bug, we say "Protect Your People." For me, that comes from my instincts as a mother wanting my children to be safe, to always feel safe. And when you apply that thinking, it opens up different avenues—as it did in the same profound way for Carol and Greg. It wasn't necessarily the incident with Joe that changed them; it was how Carol and Greg acted on it—by reaching out to me, to De-Bug, and then deciding to make the big move out of San Jose, choosing to live a whole new life. Now, we're literally family. My son and Carol and Greg's daughter got married and have three beautiful children, going on four. Joe is home, part of the family business, and getting his second chance in life.

I still remember us at De-Bug sitting on the on the porch at a retreat one time. All we needed was moonshine. And we went around asking ourselves what we wanted to see in five years. And we said: this, in every state, every city. Communities coming together to free families from the system. And all the things we talked about that night have become real. It's all come to pass. I am seventy years old now, and I am so proud to be, at this late in my life, part of something so powerful.

Philadelphia, Pennsylvania
Protect the Child, Protect the Village
William Bentley
YOUTH ART & SELF-EMPOWERMENT PROJECT HUB

Do you believe in second chances? My name is William Bentley and I was locked up and charged as an adult at the age of seventeen. This means that the district attorney, the judges, and communities of Philadelphia believe that a seventeen-year-old was such a threat to himself and peers that I needed to be sent away to an adult prison to "rehabilitate." One of *Merriam-Webster*'s definitions of "rehabilitation" is to restore someone to health. Sounds to me like *Merriam-Webster* needs some better insight on this word, because prison was never going to restore me to anything.

There is the saying that it takes a village to raise a child. But my village had its own challenges that we all were dealing with growing up.

That same village, though, is what saved me. And our village uses participatory defense to protect our youth from the decisions made about us by prosecutors and judges. The first time I was introduced to participatory defense was while I was still fighting my case while incarcerated. I was reached out to by the Youth Art & Self-Empowerment Project (YASP)—a youth-led organization that is working to end the practice of trying and incarcerating young people as adults.

At the time I connected with them, I was facing up to fifteen years in prison, and I didn't know what to do with my dilemma. The lead prosecutor and the judge had agreed with each other that they wanted to sentence me to a range of 7.5 to 15 years. I was terrified. I was lost. I was a new father, and if they got what they wanted, it was looking like I wasn't going to be there for my child's life. If I was incarcerated that long, my kid would just fall victim to the same cycle I did, my father did, and his father did.

Fortunately, the Philadelphia Community Bail Fund bailed me out, and the first thing I did was connect with YASP on the outside about my case. They supported me, encouraged me, and helped me believe that I could to change the outcome of my case. In the process, I also changed the outcome of my life.

YASP had just been through a training in participatory defense, and I was seeing the steps of the court system in real time as I was going through it. We figured out how to bring my humanity back into my courtroom. Up until that point, from arrest on and during the whole process of me going through the court system, no one ever truly talked about me, who I was. They only saw me as "No. 1162765"—that was my prison identification number. It was never introduced that I was a father, a scholar, a kid that's just trying to figure out how to navigate this thing we call life. They—the judges and prosecutors—just uplifted the mistakes I made as a kid, and never anything else.

At YASP, we worked to force them to see me as who I was, who I was becoming, where I was headed. At the participatory defense meetings, we came up with the themes we needed to communicate—my role as a father, a community leader, a valued co-worker. We listed who could best speak on each point based on their own experience with me, and we created both a social biography packet and a social biography video that my attorney could use. It felt surreal to work on a project that could and did change the outcome of my case entirely.

We used photos from when I was leading rallies for youth justice at YASP events, and in the video showed all things I did as a dad. I shared about all that I had to endure while growing up, how I had lost fourteen people close to me by the time I was seventeen. We even had clips of me facilitating the youth hub in the video.

The video in my case brought people into the court process, and they spoke while being in the community, so it took my case outside of the walls of the court. It showed—not just in my words but in the voices of people around me—that my present and future was so much more than the mistakes that defined my life since I was a child. I was no longer a career criminal, a menace to society that the DA's office was trying to paint me as. I was now a young person with a full life ahead of me, who had survived more than what may have broken the same prosecutors and judges who were trying to send me to prison. And it showed how, looking forward, I was someone whom a child depended on, a youth organizer whom a community relied on.

We turned in the video and packet, and my public defender used both to advocate for me. The YASP village was with me at every court date. I ended up not going to jail for years of my life. I was flabbergasted when the same judge and DA that were saying I had to be locked up because I was a danger to my community were forced to change their position on me. When I heard the decision, the first thing I thought about was that I wouldn't be spending any more time away from my children. I went out to eat later that night with my family and friends and just couldn't believe those years of incarceration hanging over me were gone.

Through YASP, I helped start the first youth participatory defense hub in the United States in Philadelphia. My case was one of our first victories, and we just kept going for other young people. The youth hub is exactly the same concept, just youth focused. The average age that attends our hub is fourteen to twenty-six years old. We thought it was important to have a space for young people to support each other and be supported. We see about twenty young adults a week at the youth hub.

Everyone talks about reform and prison reform. But many of the reforms today seem to leave out youth justice. That is why the youth hub in Philadelphia is so vital, since imprisonment rates for incarcerated youth are the worst in the state there.

We hold our hub meetings every Tuesday at the YASP office on the fourth floor. It's a community-based environment where you come to share free food and talk through what's the best possible way to help whoever is in need. In the room are parents, caregivers, community members, grandparents—all these different bands of people that care about you, me, and anyone else that walks through our doors. We start each meeting by setting the tone. Whoever is facilitating, which is usually a young person who has been through the system, will say, "This is a safe space, and you can share what you want."

Having people there like me and others who were formerly incarcerated and know exactly what these kids are going through is such a great asset. This village, the hub that is so vital to Philadelphia, is suffering one of the worst homicide, opioid addiction, and gun pandemics that we have ever seen. We need this badly right now.

Judges, when they sentence youths and take away their freedom, believe what they're doing is right. They go to sleep peacefully every night after sentencing humans to rot away forever.

But the logic of how that helps anyone doesn't work. If it did, why are Philadelphia homicide rates breaking records as we continue to lock up generations of youth? I believe my village is responding to the crisis in a real way, and we have living proof that this works.

An example is a young person I had helped and navigated through the hub. I supported him through meetings and court appearances when I was first out but still fighting my own case. We made a social biography video for him that had a similar impact to what mine did for me. It's making a piece of art that has drastic results. We went to every court date with him, helping him talk through life. I remember he used to have a hard time passing drug screens, so I showed him things he could do other than smoking weed. His case ended up getting transferred over to the juvenile system and was later thrown out. He had been looking at ten years in prison that got tossed out.

To see him four years later, happy and free with two beautiful daughters, helped me get that same sleep that judges do every night. But my sleep is because I helped keep a family together rather than separated.

Both he and I fought for our second chances; I am very proud to say that you should too.

Santa Clara, California
The Police Took Him from School;
We Freed Him from the Hall
Blanca Bosquez
ALBERT COBARRUBIAS JUSTICE PROJECT

I got a call one afternoon after school from my son Danny, who said he couldn't find his younger brother Rudy at school. Danny was seventeen and Rudy sixteen. They had a spot at the high school where they would meet after school so they could walk home together. They had been doing this for years, since they were both little.

I rushed to the school only to be told by someone that the police took him. No notification to the parents or anyone. Later, I obtained papers from the school showing that the detectives who questioned my son had instructed school administrators not to contact his parents. He was then taken to the police station and interrogated for several hours. Upon being detained by officers at his high school, he was denied contact with me, even after he asked for me.

At the detention center, my son supposedly confessed to the crime of robbing a taxi driver and being the mastermind behind a team who conspired to rob him. He was being charged with felony strong-armed robbery with the use of a gun. What complicates this case, and why such an allegation could not be possible, is that he was only sixteen years old and had struggled with significant mental disability ever since he was born. Although he was sixteen, his mind was that of an eight-year-old. He was born to my sister who was addicted to drugs. I adopted him shortly after he was born, but he was no different than any of my five older children. If anything, they all looked after little Rudy because he just needed the extra help. His developmental issues are at the level that he receives support and care from county agencies, and essentially requires twenty-four-hour supervision to function adequately. As a result of his challenges, he cannot verbalize much due to a speech impairment, and is currently learning to sign. This is why the notion of him masterminding anything, let alone admitting to it, seemed ridiculous.

I came to De-Bug the Sunday after my son was taken into

custody and placed in the worst unit that any juvenile could be placed in due to the charges. My son had not spent time alone anywhere, much less in juvenile hall. They placed him under suicide watch after I told them he never was without any of us adults since birth. He didn't even know how to turn the knobs on in the shower. It was the worst weekend of our lives.

I was holding a car wash for my son to raise funds for a private attorney, in the eastside of San Jose, where car washes or food sales were a common thing people would do to raise money—whether for court, bail, or a funeral. Someone came by and asked me if I had reached out to De-Bug. De-Bug was known in the community as the one place you go to that'll have your back, no matter what it might be. Got evicted, lost your job, got beaten up by police, your manager shorting you at work? People would just say go to De-Bug and they'll help you figure it out. I had known of De-Bug because I had worked with them when I was trying to change the conditions in our local juvenile hall years back when my older son was there. We marched together and would hold meetings, and they supported me and other San Jose families in challenging the conditions in juvenile hall.

But this time was a little different. It wasn't a "campaign" like changing policies. It was about the safety of my sixteen-year-old youngest who was detained far from me, and despite all I knew about organizing, I didn't know what to do with Rudy.

So I went there that Sunday afternoon after we wrapped up the car wash. There was a group of people meeting about their cases in court. I knew this feeling—of people just supporting each other. When I brought up Rudy's situation, everyone's jaw dropped. I couldn't even get through the meeting without crying. But hearing other families there, like Gail, who in spite of their own challenges could see past my tears and think through what we had to do as a community to get Rudy home, was relieving. It wasn't just about feeling my pain; by the time I left, we had clear steps to take. We discussed a game plan that really helped extract the issues that were present at that moment: Rudy's well-being inside the hall, and Rudy's representation at court the next day.

So, with the help of another mother, I sent an email to the head of the Juvenile Department of the Public Defender's Office to ensure that my son was being well-watched in custody and asked her to send the most prepared attorney to the detention hearing. I also told her we were going to bring family and supporters as well as a lot of records showing Rudy's disability and medical history so that she could help make the case that if the charges couldn't be dropped on Monday, then the judge should at least release him so he could be cared for at home.

Juvenile court is different than adult court. In Santa Clara County, the juvenile court is attached to juvenile hall. Usually, only parents or guardians are allowed inside the court, and the seats are limited—about fifteen at max, two or three rows. Then it's the DA, the defender, the young person, the probation officer, and the judge. Sometimes the judges' courtrooms have those posters that are sold to middle schoolers with inspirational sayings like "The world is yours." But it's a little trickier to pack a courtroom in juvenile court because the proceedings are usually closed, and it requires the judge to approve it.

But because the defense attorney who showed up that morning had received my email, she knew I was coming. That Monday morning, we had fifteen people show up: Rudy's brothers and sisters, grandparents, and De-Bug members. It was the detention hearing, whose purpose was to decide whether or not a young person can be released while charges are pending. In California, young people are not entitled to bail; it's all at the discretion of the probation officer or judge. I insisted on having everyone come inside the court. The attorney said she'd check in with Rudy, who was already inside as well as the judge, and if the judge okayed it, then we'd all be able to go in.

Whatever our attorney said, worked. One by one, we all filed into court and took up every seat available. Everyone's eyes were big, and I got to sit next to Rudy and hold him. He immediately cried, and so did I. It felt so good to hug him, rub his head, hold his hand. I could feel his energy fall into my body. I think it was all the stress of the separation that had hung on him since that Friday when the police picked him up from school. It was the first time he ever felt alone.

His defender made a pitch for release, and also shared some information on why the police had the wrong person. She asked if anyone in the audience wanted to speak, and my oldest son immediately stood up. He couldn't get even a word in when the tears started to flow. In his late twenties, he struggled to find the words about his baby brother, and all he could do was express how heartbroken he was at the thought of his baby brother not home with us. One by one, we spoke, and De-Bug members spoke about how they would support him to fight the charges.

My son was immediately released that day by the judge. We couldn't stop crying.

What followed while my son was out of custody was about another four months of fighting for his innocence. I made sure I had access to all of the discovery and police reports. I watched the interrogation video of him by the police. He couldn't say his address or phone number. At one point, the officer taunted him, making fun of his speech, and asked him if "there is something wrong with your mouth?" It felt like the officers were trying to take advantage of my son's condition. Interrogations are never as they are on TV shows, where the police are portrayed as trying to find the truth. With Rudy—as with most people—they were trying to build a case. I learned that those are two different goals. Any defense attorney could look at that interrogation and clearly see my son has a developmental disability, but what I was able to help point out were Rudy's mannerisms, what he was saying or trying to say. The police officers, years older than Rudy, the ones who were supposed to be adults in the situation, just ran through their questions and tried to convince Rudy he was the one that robbed the taxi driver. Then when he cried at the end, just asking to go home, asking what he did wrong, it just broke my heart.

Other De-Bug members watched that video with me. I know the purpose of viewing it was to point out anything in the video that questioned what makes a "confession," but another unspoken part of them being with me was just to help hold me together.

I also held records and documents of all of Rudy's medical history as well as school records that show he's had an IEP (Individualized Education Plan) all his school life. These records usually take a long time to obtain if an attorney has to go through the courts to get them, but I was diligent in keeping all of them, so I was able to give them to Rudy's defense attorney right away to help show his history. Presenting Rudy's history, challenging the interrogation video and police reports, and constantly meeting with his defense attorney to share all of our information and observations ultimately led to the charges being dismissed.

The dismissal of the charges was a big victory for Rudy, our family, and our De-Bug community. This road could have ended up in a different place. With the severity of the charges, Rudy could also have been prosecuted as an adult and faced prison time. Who knows what one more day in juvenile hall could've done to Rudy? But he came home. We brought him home.

5

CRIMMIGRATION

A group of about fifteen of us gathered around the big, round red table where we hold our weekly participatory defense meetings. But this wasn't our regular meetup; instead, we were all sitting on one side, facing the big screen on the opposite side, silently waiting. We were in immigration court—virtually. One of the vestiges of COVID shutting down courts in 2020 was the growth of virtual courts—ways for people to participate in and observe court hearings through online platforms. We were in the immigration hearing for Eladio, who was being held at the Immigration and Customs Enforcement (ICE) detention facility at Golden State Annex, while his mom sat anxiously in the center of our group. She had been coming to weekly meetings for four years. Just two months back, Eladio completed a seventeen-year prison sentence after being convicted as an adult for an incident that happened when he was just seventeen years old.

The months since the end of Eladio's prison sentence should have been about his long-awaited reunification with his family. They should have been dedicated to his navigating reentry to and making real the postincarceration life he had dreamed and planned from his bunk over the years. But instead, when Eladio was finally released from the California prison system, and when he walked his final steps away from the institution, he was taken to a different bus than the rest of the people being released that day. He was passed off in handcuffs from one carceral system to another: ICE detention.

That Eladio even had court and wasn't already deported was due to his family's quick action. Anticipating the transfer to ICE, they were prepared to intervene. Their calls to ICE demanding that he get his hearing stopped ICE in its tracks. The government was not expecting any intervention so it was fast-tracking Eladio's deportation. Agents had to stop the van when it was halfway to the Mexico–U.S. border and bring Eladio back so he could have his immigration court hearing, where he and his family could fight for his freedom.

Due to Eladio's immigration status, he was being targeted and punished by the nexus of two overlapping systems—the U.S. criminal legal system and the U.S. detention and deportation system. That danger zone is a particularly oppressive and heartless Venn diagram that organizers and immigrant rights advocates have labeled "crimmigration."

We first saw the crimmigration terror years ago when a long-time De-Bug member, Jacob, was being held in a federal detention center and was told he was going to be deported to his home country of Colombia because of a prior conviction he pled to. That charge was a vandalism felony from graffiti he had done when he was still a teen. Since then, Jacob had become a father, and his kids and entire family—his whole life—were located in San Jose.

It was only when we reached out to immigration attorneys that we learned how uniquely vulnerable people like Jacob and Eladio are when in ICE custody due to contact with the criminal court system. Attorneys who we knew were tremendous advocates for the immigrant communities, who attended marches and rallies for immigrant rights, wouldn't take Jacob's case. They all kept using the same code word: they'd say the case was too "complicated." Years later, we came to understand the political undercurrent baked into the term "complicated." It signaled a much larger problematic backdrop that came up even in advocacy spaces: the false dichotomy of the "good" versus "bad" immigrant. Good immigrants didn't get criminal convictions, were adhering to the American Dream, and could thus be palatably absorbed into the American polity. But immigrants who got arrested, prosecuted, and convicted in the criminal legal system were not deserving of America, or in some cases, even the support of the immigrant rights movement. In some circles, even immigrant rights movement circles, they argued that national immigration reform required distance from the "bad" immigrant.

This meant that even in Santa Clara County, a community rich in immigrant rights advocacy, Jacob was too . . . "complicated." But of course, the crimmigration system was based on a nonsensical premise, even from its own self-described purposes. The immigration system isn't, allegedly, supposed to be an extra punishment mechanism of the criminal legal system. But that is precisely how the systems conspire. In this collusion, every conviction for an immigrant, even for something like graffiti, can turn into a possible deportation. For Jacob, and for the movement around us, we needed the immigrant rights movement to understand the irrationality of the bad-immigrant trope, and how that cut against the entirety of the movement. Plus, the worthy immigrant versus undeserving immigrant frame required them to assume the criminal legal system had integrity and validity. That was a bridge too far, as advocates in the immigrant community had witnessed racist policing and prosecution across communities for years. Unlawful arrests, overcharging, and racially disproportionate sentences were a widespread and common experience of immigrant communities' interaction with the local criminal legal system. That analysis, combined with families like Jacob's engaging with local immigrant rights advocates, helped to change the atmosphere in Santa

Clara County. It was no longer about drawing an imaginary line between who deserves protection from ICE and who doesn't; it became about our movement protecting *all* community members from detention and deportation.

As a result, our county became one of the first in the nation to stop county cooperation with ICE, halting the process of the local jail notifying and transferring immigrant community members to ICE, regardless of charge or conviction.

But the climbs to these wins are steep, and even with certain protections against ICE in a local community, the crimmigration threat is real and ever present when an immigrant faces a criminal charge or conviction. So if the systems of separation are expanded, it means the participatory defense protections need to grow to be responsive to protect our people from crimmigration attacks.

Through Jacob's own advocacy, his family, his community here at De-Bug, and an incredible attorney named Angie Junck, who had been focusing on this crimmigration intersection at the time, we were eventually able to extract him from federal detention, prevent his deportation, and return him to his kids. A lesson we learned from Jacob's case was that what may feel like a win to the person and family in the criminal court—a plea to a much lesser charge, or a sentence that doesn't mean more jail time—could absolutely tank the person's chances in immigration court. Jacob, for example, may not have had to spend all that time in immigration detention had he not taken a plea that left him susceptible in immigration court. The lawyers in criminal court are often not thinking about immigration consequences, so what may look like the best result in that arena could devastate the person in the immigration court context. And immigration attorneys are often not familiar with the criminal court that caused the person to have to face a possible deportation in the first place. These attorneys from two different court worlds often don't communicate with each other, even if they represent the same person. So for immigrant families, participatory defense in crimmigration is navigating, strategizing, and disrupting two systems simultaneously.

Eladio's case is called, and he appears on the screen. He's in the room in the detention center, where detainees take turns sitting positioned in front of a camera, holding a landline phone to their ear to listen to the court and U.S. government lawyers talk about their futures. The lawyer for the government, Eladio's attorney, and the judge are all on screens too, and share appearances in the middle box when they each speak.

Though Eladio is usually soft-spoken, he sounds noticeably quieter today. He looks sleepy. The judge asks him a few basic questions around the status of his case, then sets a date for the new hearing. Eladio's whole screen time is under five minutes. He stands up and walks off-camera, leaving the seat for the next man to sit down and get processed. Eladio is on the fourteenth day of a hunger strike he is participating in along with others detained in ICE facilities at Golden State Annex and Mesa Verde. They are protesting the inhumane treatment in these prisons and are drawing on one of the most powerful historic movement tactics that the incarcerated, the oppressed, and the colonized have used for generations across the globe: a hunger strike. Eladio and the others detained are literally putting their lives on the line to push for dignity and basic human rights as they still face the system that is trying to banish them from this country. He explained to his family that he is going on the hunger strike for others, so they won't have to face the same conditions he is surviving through.

We sign off the virtual court after Eladio leaves the screen. His mother had noted the next hearing date, and will show up to the participatory defense meeting to strategize next steps. Because of Jacob, and hub leaders across the country like the authors in this section, she and Eladio will be lifted up by the support, wisdom, and experiences of other families who were in the same exact criminal court/immigration court crosshairs they find themselves in. They will share their knowledge and ideas, and Eladio's family will know that while they are fighting against a two-headed monster, they've got backup, not just in San Jose but from hubs across the country, to reunify their families.

Just weeks after the virtual hearing, Eladio won a bond hearing and was finally returned home. Instead of being deported, or confined to a cell, he is sitting at that same red table, alongside his mom and the other families doing their weekly updates and next steps. He still has a deportation case to beat, but is able to fight it at home with his family and with community by his side.

This section highlights the many challenges of navigating the maze-like trap of the crimmigration system. But it also shares stories, like that of Eladio and his family, of communities collectively navigating, taking on, and beating the threats of detention and deportation.

San Mateo, California
My Mother versus ICE
Sarait Escorza
SAN MATEO HUB

As an immigrant daughter, I have always had to look out for my family, perhaps because I was one of the first in my family to pick up English or because, as the oldest of the girl children, I grew right into that role. Regardless, there was an innate instinct to protect my loved ones just like many of us do.

In January 2010 during a winter break visit from college at my parents' house in East Palo Alto, California, I came to realize that despite my educated background and ability to speak English, none of that helped to stop my seventeen-year-old sister from being taken by the police to juvenile hall. I still remember that moment vividly. I heard the doorbell ring, and dogs were barking in the background as I walked up to open the door, wondering who could possibly be there. We had just celebrated the holidays with our family and weren't expecting anyone. When I opened the door, I gasped in disbelief when I saw two men in police uniform standing there. As you can imagine, the twenty-year-old in me proceeded to ask, "What are you doing here?" and one of the officers responded, "We are looking for you!" I was shocked. Shortly, as the officers were attempting to take me, my sister walked into the room; they realized they had the wrong person and went inside our living room to handcuff her.

I immediately asked why they were taking her and what had happened, but they didn't respond. Unfortunately, this was not the first time my sister had had run-ins with the police, but seeing her being ripped away from us in that moment made me feel helpless. I didn't know what our legal rights were, and as someone without legal status, it crossed my mind that anyone else in the house could be taken as well.

I don't recall how soon we found out that my sister had a detention hearing, but it sure felt like an eternity. My mother drove us to the juvenile hall in San Mateo County, all the way up in the hills. You would be dismayed at the breathtaking view that ironically is also the most isolating and dehumanizing place for our youth.

In the courtroom, I sat next to my mom as usual to help translate. I couldn't find less technical terms for half of the words uttered by the judge, but as the hearing came to an end, the words that struck me the most were "I am ordering an ICE hold." I had a flashback to all the news coverage and marches by immigrant rights organizers I had seen on TV; I had heard that term before and I knew what that meant. I froze. I didn't know how to tell my mother that my sister could possibly be taken by ICE. My voice cracked as I told my mom what the judge had ordered. My mother and I could not figure out how to tell the awful news to the rest of our family, especially since our immigration status was not something we talked about.

It was heartbreaking to return to school with a piece of me missing. I could not concentrate in class thinking about when my sister would be picked up and what I could possibly do to help keep our family together.

One day as I was trying to write an essay for class, I received an email from one of my dear mentors and close friends, Charisse Domingo, who paved the way for me to get into community organizing back when I had no idea what that was. The email was an introduction to the chief of the Private Defender Program (San Mateo's version of a public defender's office) to figure out the name of the attorney that was previously representing my sister and of course, to raise the obvious immigration concerns. When I called my mom, she shared how another mom had told her about these Sunday meetings in San Jose and she decided to go to get some help.

I didn't know what we were doing but I did know that I trusted Charisse and I trusted my mother's lead, so I jumped right in as part of the support team. Sunday after Sunday, I'd get these email notes from the meetings and during the week I talked to my mother to make sure we got through the to-do lists that were being generated on Sundays. Sometimes, I came home for the week from school, even if it meant missing school, to attend hearings, meet with my sister's immigration attorney, and be there for my mother.

My mother. This woman with the brown sun-kissed skin tone, who was five feet tall and a house cleaner. Though she had just a few English words in her back pocket that got her by, this woman had a fierce power within her. There were no barriers or limitations that would get in the way of her freeing her daughter. She transmitted the energy that she picked up at the Sunday meetings with other families and sparked the light of hope in me. We were no longer afraid to put ourselves out there, defy those we were taught to respect as "authority," and question the way the system was designed.

My mom and I had to work diligently on the next steps from the participatory defense meetings. Some of those next steps included: connecting with the juvenile attorney in San Mateo, who was the best person to provide information around my sister's case; securing an immigration attorney to do a legal consultation and determine any potential relief options to stop the deportation; following up and maintaining constant communication with both attorneys; attending juvenile court hearings; informing my sister not to sign any documents from ICE; gathering documentation for the U visa application, and most important, keeping my sister's strength and faith up. Sometimes criminal defense attorneys and immigration attorneys work on different paths, and sometimes a decision in a criminal court may undermine opportunities for freedom in immigration court. We had to keep everyone in a united front.

After eight long months of uncertainty, and constant hard work put in by my mother, our community, and her legal support, we learned that my sister's U visa application was approved. That meant that her deportation order would be lifted. This piece of paper that validated my sister's existence in this country was her way back home and would end her immigration proceedings. At this point, my sister was detained at an ICE group home in Fullerton, California. Though we thought the nightmare was over, we still had to jump through another hoop. Before we could take my sister home, social workers had to inspect our home and make sure it was suitable for her—as if the time we had been separated had not been enough. After a couple of visits, they determined she could come home.

Sometime in August, we made our way to Fullerton, in Southern California, which must have been a six or seven-hour drive. When we got to the group home, my mother and I walked to what appeared to be the main office and waited for maybe thirty to forty minutes. As I watched my sister walk up to us with a bag in her hand, tears rolled down my eyes. This day seemed impossible. It was the determination and empowerment of my mother that brought my sister home!

The overpowering experience that someone with no immigration legal expertise can take down a whole system that wanted to destroy one family is hard to put into words. We're conditioned to be deferential to those with the degrees, but in this case, a mother along with community support made a statement that we would not let ICE win this fight. Little did I know this experience would be the beginning of a transformative and life-changing movement journey in which others like my sister could be liberated and reunited with their families.

With the trust and confidence of my De-Bug family, I helped launch the San Mateo County Participatory Defense hub in September 2016. The origins of this hub were fundamentally cemented on the core value of this model: that families are the experts and those closest to the issue can and will make systemic change. Both Lourdes Best and I, longtime East Palo Alto residents and community organizers, started leading meetings right behind St. Francis of Assisi Church in East Palo Alto. Seeing the growth and the ripple impacts of participatory defense in the larger community is quite invigorating and priceless. We have ripped back our families, loved ones, and community members from the claws of the evil system intended to incarcerate our people and have reclaimed the courts by infusing community power and bringing a sense of transformation and empowerment to families that were at their lowest points in their lives. Every family that walks into our participatory defense meetings is a reminder that when community comes together we're invincible. Being able to witness families who fight with such resiliency and are invested in the well-being of their loved ones, determined to hold systems and court players accountable, is what drives me. In San Mateo County alone, we have been able to save over 300 years of incarceration over the last six years and we're going for more because loved ones are better off at home with their families.

Los Angeles, California
Crimmigration Avenue
Phal Sok

LOS ANGELES HUB

It was a sunny morning and as good a day as any to wake up. I was in my mid-thirties and I was supposed to be released from state prison, but by the end of the day, I was in another place, caged by a different system. What started as being ready to walk out the gate became nothing more than a memory of the streets, a place I last saw at seventeen years old.

I knew I was getting closer to this moment day by day. As days overlapped one to the next, I had to wrestle with having an immigration hold and what that meant. I had been locked up for so long that I had an "INS hold," a piece of paper that said I could not go free without the state calling immigration agents, a product of those agreements with the Immigration and Naturalization Service three decades before. If you know the feeling of wanting to be wrong, I wanted to be wrong. But on that sunny morning, the system wouldn't let me be. The prison held me for ICE.

Ronald Reagan may be remembered as the president who gave green cards through amnesty, but he is less remembered for his role as an architect of the deportation machinery of today. That blame often falls on Barack Obama with his community legacy as "Deporter-in-Chief," but he couldn't have risen to that fame without the foundation laid by his predecessors, including Reagan. Nearly four decades ago, while amnesty green cards were being processed under Reagan's watch, a system of collaboration between the criminal legal and immigration systems was unfolding. The Alien Criminal Apprehension Program was born, and California became part of the so-called Five State Criminal Alien Model.

Immigration and Customs Enforcement, aka ICE, did not always exist. Back in the 1980s, enforcement was handled by the Immigration and Naturalization Service (INS). While it was issuing amnesty green cards, it was making agreements with California's law enforcement agencies to identify, process, and deport noncitizens who had police contact or ended up in jail or prison. For anyone who got caught in those crosshairs, where even the smallest police contact became deportations, they got stranded on Crimmigration Avenue. In the summer of 2015, I crossed that intersection while Obama was in office, and ICE was in full effect targeting those of us who had been locked up.

If I had been born here in the United States, I would have walked out as a parolee on my way to Los Angeles before sunset. Instead, I was put into a different room and greeted by a new set of chains and locks. I was taken into a van and driven through the prison gate, where I got to see people walk free. I was a migrant being taken to "immigration detention" to get deported. I was shackled in a caged van driving across Crimmigration Avenue, taking the exit out of prison as only a paper parolee.

This moment in my life was the culmination of the many events of history's past. I was walking a road that was laid by racism and hatred. It was tied to the creation of a country built for the "free white person" when the first Congress came together to say who could be a citizen. It was tied to the Chinese Exclusion Act and California playing host to "coolie" clubs. It was tied to "yellow peril." It was tied to over two centuries of oppression against non-whites. Federal courts have repeatedly said immigration law is the second most complex body of law in the United States, second only to tax code. For those of us who end up trapped in the crimmigration system, ways out are few and far between. My success at threading that needle would come with extreme odds.

Before I left the prison gate, I had already studied immigration law and saw that I had no way out, except through a pardon. I had accepted the fate that I had no legal outcome besides a deportation order since the Immigration and Nationality Act mandated my deportation. It meant I had to do what I could to get physically freed before a plane could come to take me. The one thing I had in my favor was that I was not a citizen of a country that readily accepted American deportees. This meant it was more difficult to send me back, and so I had the possibility of having a temporary reprieve of being free.

I was held in immigration lockup for eight months. I had been taken up and down the West Coast while they tried to deport me. I had a deportation order on the books for six months. Under federal case law, they had to decide whether to try to hold me indefinitely or let me go. I could see it was going to be another sunny day out the window overlooking the streets just outside the walls that kept me in. Before this day was over, though, I would be sitting on a curb, free but unfree. I can't tell you what it was like for me to be outside for the first time as an adult. I had last set foot on pavement without leg irons when I was seventeen. Although I would get to stand next to my brother that day without prison blues, I was not free. I had a deportation order that was just waiting to get used. It was just a matter of time, this I knew.

Freedom came and then freedom went. I had been out for less than three months when I got a letter from ICE. It said they wanted to follow up with me on my supervision. I was instructed to check in at the office on a different unscheduled date. It just didn't feel right. I showed up as instructed and indeed they took me back in.

But this time, I was not alone. I had built a community. I connected with a church, I met people from nonprofits, and I started what would become a most valuable friendship with someone doing immigration policy work—my friend Carlos. I had the beginnings of a participatory defense outcome in the works.

So off I go back into a local jail that had a contract with ICE. To understand where my mind was at, I must say that I was ready to go. I had spent the last month being out saying goodbyes and living under duress I had never before felt. I was tired of being unfree. I was depleted and I just wanted to move on. But that community I had built showed up unexpectedly. They came to visit. They took my calls. They came to say they didn't know what to do but if there was the possibility of me doing something to stay with them, they wanted that. Over late-night calls and multiple visits, we came to an agreement. I had asked ICE when I was going to be put on a plane and they said in two weeks. I made an agreement that if two weeks went by and I was still not gone I would pull a Hail Mary and file in the federal courts using the legal skills I taught myself while incarcerated. Two weeks passed and I filed. My flight was canceled, and I was sent to Louisiana.

I held on to my agreement and I kept at it. I had some back and forth with the federal courts and eventually the federal government reopened my immigration case. This meant my case would not be heard in the federal courts and my claims would never see publication. But this also meant that I was going back to the immigration courts in Los Angeles. This also meant an opportunity for my community to step in. At that time, another piece of case law said that I was eligible for a bond hearing since I had been physically released for some time. I filed for a bond hearing and my community showed up to tell the judge what only the community could tell him. In the end, a bond was granted and paid for by my community. I would see the streets again, courtesy of my community.

The journey from here was one of uncertainty. I still had to go back to immigration court. I still had an open deportation case. Immigration law was still clear that I had no way out except through a pardon from the governor. Now that the forty-fifth president was on his way into office, all bets were off in getting any kind of break. I had no choice but to get a pardon, a power move that had been unheard of for my situation. I could not find a pardon given to someone that had just been released from prison, especially to stop a deportation. Pardons had been granted, of course, but to people who had been out for a long time, a decade or longer. There was no road map or recipe to follow. I just had to do it.

At that time, I thought of pardons as a political process, as a black box that nobody really understood. As I settled back into my community, I kept searching for some way to get to the governor. In the end, I would reach him with the help of my community. My friend Carlos and other organizers called me in to join the immigrant rights movement, and that is what built my personal and political presence. That presence is what led to getting a pardon. I cannot emphasize enough that my pattern of success always came with community.

My bond was paid at the end of November 2016. I walked out just days after the Electoral College turned red and the media was full of hateful rhetoric against immigrants. There was no better time to be fighting deportation. I returned to Los Angeles to the community-based transitional housing program I had previously lived at to regroup. I had taken up the invitation to join the immigrant rights movement. The community came forward and elevated me, as someone who was fighting deportation for having a criminal record that the state deemed violent. What the system saw, community did not see. Community saw a human being in need, a friend in need.

The more I settled in, the more opportunities kept coming to build my leadership. I got involved in all kinds of campaigns and plugged in with various local, statewide, and national spaces. I became well-loved, admired, and respected, so much so that opportunities arose for me to have representation before the governor's office with a prestigious seal. I was able to get support letters from community members, community organizations, academics, professionals, politicians, and more. By the time my pardon application was filed, I had amassed support from every level except the White House—from boots on the ground all the way to Congress. I had built friendships with people who would talk to the governor's office for me, enough connections that we had support next to the governor's ear.

In my mind, though, the pinnacle of the campaign was a pardon video specifically made for the governor. I didn't start out knowing anything about social bio videos and nobody at Silicon Valley De-Bug knew me, but the community brought us together. This video was a work of love and ambition. So many people showed up to be filmed that not everyone could be in the final piece. So much was said and captured that the team had to buy extra hard drives to store the terabytes of footage we were amassing.

As I watched all the filming unfold and listened to all the people that showed up one after the other, I had an opportunity to experience something we don't get much of. I got to hear my community articulate what I meant to them in their own words, their choice of body movements, and most of all, their display of emotion off camera. The things I heard people say, as if they had an audience with the governor at that point in time, were very much refreshing for the soul: Moments when people smiled as they reminisced about an encounter we had. Moments of human-to-human interaction revisualized in their mind's eye. Moments like when my brother gave me a piece of my family history, giving me a deeper understanding of how they got to their first steps in America. The moments we often don't get to realize how much we mean to each other.

In the end, final production would produce a short film nearing a half-hour long. It would send a clear message, through the lens of participatory defense, of who I was and what community wanted. By this time, we had spent about a year preparing my application and building political support. It was time to file. It was time for us to be heard.

In August 2018, the governor's office called. I had been granted a pardon. I hadn't even been home for two years. Community celebrated and community rejoiced. It was a moment when people got to feel joy and not tears, a win and not a loss. I had received a pardon that was thought to be impossible. Based on then-governor Brown's patterns of pardons, it was also out of order. He had a pattern of issuing clemency around Easter and Christmas. I received mine in time to go to immigration court in November 2018. Pardon in hand, my deportation case was closed at that hearing. If Governor Brown had waited until Christmas, the outcome may not have been as sweet. If community had not come together to make the impossible possible, who knows where I would be today.

There is an absolute and definite reality that I would have been deported if things didn't work out as they did. When I was taken back in, Cambodia had agreed to take me and made it official. Documentation was on the books, ready for one-way travel. I would have landed in a country I had never before set foot in. I was born in Thailand, but I do not have Thai registration and so no legal Thai identity. I was born in a refugee camp, a product of humanitarian aid, a product of war. My Cambodian parents made me a Cambodian citizen by blood. Borders exist all over the world. My parents happened to cross one that is on the other side of the earth. They would fit the derogation of being "border hoppers."

Fortunately for me, my outcome was one that made our community happy. This "border hopper" tale was one of many, but also one of the few to hold a joyous ending. I don't see how I could have done it entirely on my own or with just a "legal team." Even if there was some other way, I doubt I would have ventured it. For me, participatory defense has always been to stand together, to win together. That pardon was not just for me—it was for our community.

Knoxville, Tennessee
Aiming the Activism
Imani Mfalme Shu'la
COMMUNITY DEFENSE OF EAST TENNESSEE HUB

Growing up under an activist and freedom fighter while watching the prison system repeatedly take my loved ones away made me hate the system and hate racism growing up. I realized slavery is the root of this state in more ways than one. The for-profit prisons in Tennessee are the plantations of our time. Each courthouse in America is a slave ship transporting people to bondage under the illusion of public safety. Yet, when you look at the parts of the state that had the most slaves, most of them are close to a prison. So as we travel those long, winding roads in Tennessee to the prisons, we will pass several cotton fields, beautiful when in bloom, but effed up to look at and know our ancestor's blood fertilized that soil, and our peoples' souls continue to make the prison-industrial complex fruitful.

In my own life, prison has harmed my relationship with my brothers, friends, and family that went in. I watched my brothers go away, and it became so routine that, at a certain point, I didn't even cry anymore when one of my brothers went to prison. I remember being close with my brother Rico before he went away. I was a teenager, and it was easier to put him in the back of my mind to numb the hurt. Like, I made a whole person I loved and cared for disappear to cope.

Twelve years later, he came home. I had changed, he had changed, and although I love him, it's changed. I miss the bond we used to have but not sure we can ever get it back. So my entire life I had fought against the carceral system, but in 2016, I was introduced to a new way I could organize to protect our people.

In May of that year, I was invited to a community training on participatory defense coordinated by the Knox County Public Defender's Office. I had a lot of free time on my hands because I was off work due to being in chemo treatment for breast cancer. So I wanted to find something to do with all the time I had to distract me from the battle and pain I was going through.

I was absolutely blown away by what was being shared by these people from California. They came and told us their stories as if they were watching our lives, stories of police brutality, harassment, systemic and socioeconomic disparities, and how it affected their lives. And while the start of those stories were completely familiar, what got me was how they were taking control of those stories and how they ended. They shared how they could affect the outcomes of cases through their coordinated actions. It was the specific actions that pulled me in. There were actual steps that anyone could take to have an impact on a case. That was so refreshing to me. After wading through the water for so long, this finally felt like a way to rise. I remember them talking about court watching as a strategy that, from memory, I knew worked because I had seen it before. But to be intentional about the coordination of it in a way to impact the outcome of a case blew me away. They described how court watching at trial could be done in collaboration with the defense attorney, how taking notes of what testimony or evidence was resonating with the jury, then sharing that daily with the defense attorney so she could use it in real time, was a light switch going off in me. That was the first time I realized that the quality of your defense didn't necessarily have to be linked to how big a check you could write, but rather to actual knowledge on how to navigate this system. I looked at these women and thought, wow, they are sharing this knowledge that we can then turn into power. And they weren't lawyers. They were mothers and families who were fighting for their loved ones and drew from their experiences to do so.

At the same time, I was mad. It hit me that no matter how many degrees my mom had or how smart I thought I was, the only way we felt we could fight in court was through a lawsuit. So here I am with this feeling of newfound hope, ready to get to it.

I immediately bought into participatory defense and thought about what I'm sure many of us felt then. The room was filled with about thirty to forty people from my hometown—some formerly incarcerated individuals, pastors, youth program advocates, activists, and organizers. I thought to myself, It could have changed so much if we had had this tool set a long time ago. Then, I started thinking about how I instinctively participated in my own defense. Still, with this filled-out approach I probably would have been able to not only get my charges dismissed but advocate for no court costs and hold the system accountable.

We created an independent group that we named Community Defense of East Tennessee (CDET). Knoxville is 17 percent Moors. I say Moor because we were never "Black" until we came to these shores in chains. We were mainly identified by the lands we lived in; some in North Africa were called Moors, and at one time in history, the Moors ruled, so instead of placing myself and my identity on the enslaver's terms, I chose to identify with my ancestors who were conquerors. And it was important to us that it was those of us who have been directly impacted by the criminal justice system and the deeply rooted racism in the South that we were the ones leading, shaping, and directing how participatory defense was going to be in our city.

This is the root of the authenticity of participatory defense. This is a movement for the people. This is for the mothers, sisters, grandmothers, wives, and partners fighting for their loved ones to come home. That's why our first principle of participatory defense is that families need to be centered—create, decide, follow through, and lead.

I was used to various people in the community calling when people felt there had been an injustice. Then, Knoxville city councilwoman Amelia Parker reached out and said she had a case that needed support. She told me that a man named Raymond, an immigrant from Liberia, was charged by the police and needed help. So we invited Raymond to our weekly meeting.

I remember him coming in looking shaken, like he wasn't sure if he should take the next step because he might fall. His body language told the story even louder; he was crouched over as he was sitting there, as I've seen many Moor men do and try to shrink themselves in space because if not, they are considered a threat. The expression on his face was a look of uncertainty, but at that time, I think it was more so the hesitancy of being vulnerable among so many people he didn't know. Looking at him when he first came reminded me of how the system has defeated, demeaned, abused, and oppressed so many Moor people. You would never know this man survived a civil war in Liberia and was a professor at the local university.

I knew Raymond was trying to shrink himself because I was once in those shoes. I've always been a fighter and never backed down from a fight. Although that has only sometimes worked out in my favor, learning the skills of participatory defense helped me identify how to target. So I've always had the gun and the ammunition. I was just lost in the direction I needed to shoot. For instance, one of the times I was charged in a case that ended in dismissal because of an illegal search, I thought if I had had this knowledge and tools, I could have not only challenged the charges, which I did, but I would have had a way to fight and target the systemic issues that led to me getting that charge. Even though I knew we were profiled, I didn't know how to fight that. I knew that they illegally detained and arrested my passenger but didn't know how to hold them accountable or, at the very least, how to document our experience. As it turned out, I received a letter from the DA's office that one of the officers involved was criminally charged in his own case, and all the cases he was involved in were being reviewed. If I had had the participatory defense lens then, I would have made this into a community campaign to educate, empower, embolden, and support other community members affected by this. There would have been accountability, not just being glad the case was dismissed.

Raymond later told me that when he first came in, he thought,

Is this really going to help? I and the other community members there were giving him the next steps of action and ideas he could take in reference to his case. For instance, he could go through his police report and document the errors he saw, set up a meeting with his attorney, and write down his questions to prepare himself for his appointment. These steps may seem insignificant, but when an organized person walks into an attorney's office, the process is less overwhelming and can be more productive for everyone involved. He went to the meeting with information he wanted the attorney to know immediately to put up a strong defense, and had his list of questions for the attorney so he knew they were on the same page. From the participatory defense meetings, he also understood what the next court hearings would be about, so they weren't a complete mystery. The stakes were high for Raymond. If convicted, he was potentially facing deportation.

Raymond began attending weekly meetings regularly, and it's my belief that as he saw other families going through the same system and saw a community of people supporting them, he began to grow bolder and more comfortable, stating that he was wronged. His cousin Kai also attended the meetings as support, and he was the opposite of Raymond, being very outspoken from the very beginning, attending weekly meetings and candidly speaking out about all the injustices we face as a people. One of the first things we asked Raymond to do was look over his police report. As we looked at the police report, Raymond would identify the lies the troopers put together to attempt to justify the abuse he and his family suffered during a traffic stop.

We also started to prepare him for an attorney meeting. Call it fate or just that we live in a more connected city, but Raymond had hired the very same attorney that had represented one of my brothers before. At that time, my brother's mother was attending meetings to get Rico out, so we were able to tell Raymond about our experiences with the attorney and how to navigate that relationship positively. I've noticed that some attorneys are intimidated by our presence; some of the reasons they give the people they represent are baseless and have nothing to do with how we organize. The attorneys that have openly welcomed us understand the power of community and understand we are not trying to do their job, only trying to support a community member that ordinarily would be isolated and alone in this process.

When meeting with his lawyer, Raymond made sure to ask about how the criminal case would impact his immigration status. We had seen many times when someone would take a plea hoping to get the case over with as soon as possible, without considering the collateral damage of the conviction.

I noticed the more Raymond attended the meetings and the more he listened to other families, the more he began to come out of his shell. It was as if he began to let go of the stigma of shame from this situation and embraced that this was not a reflection of who he was but an ugly reflection of the inherent racism and injustice that exists in our society. By the time his case was concluded, he was ready to raise "THE FIST" against injustice.

Supporting him to complete his social biography packet allowed me to see Raymond for who he truly was, and that ultimately was the goal of the packet—to demonstrate to the court who he was and what he meant to the community. I learned that he had survived a civil war in his home country and that he was indeed a freedom fighter. He was an accomplished world scholar and had a worldview of what integrated human relationships looked like. He had written a book, and he was a very complex and layered individual. However, the more we met each week, I realized no matter the knowledge this man had, the world experience, and the accolades, the system would find a way to dwarf any honors and distinction with its strategic, predatory, oppressive nature. This man who literally survived a civil war had come to America and been beaten, abused, caged, and treated like an animal and did not know he had the ammo to fight back for himself . . . until he met us. The key here is fighting back for himself. Yes, he knew to hire an attorney, but when he was empowered and gained knowledge, in my opinion he began to gain his dignity, capability, self-determination, and everything else that was taken from him on the side of the highway that day. He started his path to liberation.

Raymond is everything about participatory defense—how someone enters our space abused by the system, having little to no trust with the actors in the system, including their own attorneys at times, but finds trust in the community process to fight back. Raymond was fully ready for his critical court date. He had created the most comprehensive social bio CDET had ever seen and had over ten people travel from other parts of the state, with his wife traveling from another country to attend court. He had letters from his family, his friends, students, colleagues, and community members. Raymond and his wife had recently completed a home study for an adoption process, which was also put in. This study contained all the information the adoption agency would need to say this family passes the criteria for adoption. We put family photos and a few of his wedding photos in his social bio. We put in his accomplishments, and we even had a hard copy of the book he authored inside. This bio was so thorough and complete that the attorneys didn't want to give it back when everything was over. We tried to keep it as an example for other family members, but they did not want to return it. Imagine that—a tool created by Raymond and the community is now something attorneys want to hold on to for future reference.

On the day of the court hearing, we all showed up and were fully prepared to give statements of support on Raymond's behalf.

Raymond had given copies of his social biography packet to his attorneys, and we waited nervously for his name to be called. I remember looking at him, his family, and his supporters as I always do when in court with someone to see how I can be present for them. The looks of determination on his family's faces were fierce. I could tell they were ready to go to war for him, and it was all placed in the love they held for him. Finally, his name was called; his attorney approached the DA, giving him the social biography packet. Then they talked, and Raymond's attorney walked away and asked Raymond to follow him into a room. They returned, and Raymond informed us that his charges would be dropped if he did community service and received no new charges for a short period of time. Once the DA stood up to tell the judge the agreement, I remember him stating that Raymond was a man doing positive things in his community, and he felt that with the conditions, he was comfortable dismissing the charges. Accepting these conditions removed the possibility of deportation that could accompany a conviction. We knew that Raymond should have walked away that day without any charges or conditions but understood and were told that they couldn't just let him off scot-free; it would not look good for the officers involved. Just another day in the injustice system, but for Raymond and his family, it was a win. He was able to do his community service with CDET, and finally, all his charges were dropped. The threat of deportation was beaten.

Now Raymond is helping to build CDET—leading meetings, supporting families, attending protests, and speaking. That person who first came through the door is now gone. He's like a ferocious lion. Now he shares his experiences with other communities like ours who are thinking about starting participatory defense. I'm glad he made a choice to continue to fight as many of us do. We are fighting for ourselves and a better world for the people we love.

We are a family in our Knoxville participatory defense hub. We go to each other's houses, eat, pray, and are present in each other's high points and lowest moments. Our organization is built around that kind of kinship. Our freedom is tied to each other's. Our community is growing stronger because we have to keep pushing.

6

POSTCONVICTION

When Salah stepped into the meeting, he reached into his bag and dropped a beat-up manila folder overflowing with legal documents onto the table. His son Malik's life was in there. The folder was heavy with the weight of the years in prison it promised. It landed with a thud.

Just weeks after his eighteenth birthday, Malik was given what amounted to a life sentence. He had taken a plea after the judge forewarned that if the case went to trial his sentence could get even worse if it reached him afterward.

Salah was the only person in the court pews when his child was sentenced to life in prison. The judge banged his gavel, Malik was brought back to holding, Salah was told to clear the courtroom, and the judge vanished behind a door behind the dais. Malik's attorney gave Salah the relevant paperwork; then he walked out of court in a daze. Salah recounted this experience while giving his updates to bring us all up to speed on his son's case. The room was still, and we could tell from his eyes that he was reliving the horror of the memory. It was his first time at De-Bug, and he didn't know it yet, but in the years to come, it would become home base in his fight against the future that was cemented by that awful day in court.

It had been several months since the sentencing and Salah wanted to fight for the freedom of his son. But how to overcome a ruling from a judge that sounded so final? The question introduced us to the long-standing struggle, led by those inside prison, for postconviction freedom. There are a lot of manila folders—some gathering dust in closets or bunkers—waiting to be opened, interrogated, refuted.

Salah came regularly to those weekly meetings and, together with the group, explored all possibilities. They went over every sheet in Malik's folder, reading transcripts and reviewing the original police reports and witness statements. Malik was part of a group that ended up in a fight in a restaurant, though he was not inside the restaurant when it occurred. One of the boys he came with unexpectedly—and tragically—shot another teen. Malik was charged with felony murder—a charge that means if more than one person is involved in a felony, and one of the participants kills someone, everyone involved in the felony suffers the same punishment, even if they didn't kill anyone. The teenagers were also given gang enhancements, a device prosecutors use to allege the act was done to benefit a gang, and greatly expands the sentencing exposure. Unsurprisingly, it's almost exclusively used on Black and Brown people.

Just like other families seeking postconviction freedom, Salah looked into appeals, commutations, early parole possibilities. Families approaching appellate attorneys were usually first met with some head scratching or skepticism. The appeal attorneys were used to ordering transcripts, sifting through court paperwork, and writing briefs. The notion of families offering their observations of court proceedings or their analyses of cases was not expected in their practice. But many appeal attorneys ended up appreciating the insight families were able to provide about their cases. Attorneys only worked within the confines of what appeared in the transcripts, but families could give the context and nuance that might not show up in black and white. The notes families were taking in court and their email exchanges with trial attorneys turned out to have actionable value in winning appeals.

Salah and Malik tried it all as months and years passed. Salah became an uncle-type figure at De-Bug. He attended our marches and rallies demanding police and DA accountability. When we were fighting for an end to draconian mandatory sentences like the ones that Malik was doing time for, he spoke powerfully as a father.

One of the young artists that came to De-Bug drew a mural of Salah speaking at a rally. At our center, to lift up that the leaders and freedom fighters who inspire us also walk among us, we laced the walls with renderings of family members who came to participatory defense meetings. That way, whenever someone new came to De-Bug and wanted to know what we were about, they saw the Salah mural. We would share the story of Malik and Salah as a way to give life to the decades of struggle against irrational laws like the felony murder rule, and the lengthy prison sentences that had decimated families. We would also share the political history that shaped his sentence. Malik was caught in the wake of California laws formed in the late 1990s that criminalized Black and Brown youth as "superpredators" and ballooned prison numbers. We would talk about Proposition 21, a ballot initiative that allowed district attorneys to directly file youth into adult court and expanded mandatory minimums and gang enhancements. It passed even though youth justice groups fought heroically against it. One of Malik's co-defendants, at fourteen years old, was the youngest person ever at the time to face a life sentence in California due to Proposition 21. For years after that destructive proposition, we would see droves of youth of color criminalized, imprisoned, and ripped from their families as a result of fear-mongering politics from that era. "Charges and sentences are reflections of political moments" we would say when people looked at the mural. That's why the organizing outside of the courts was so critical to what happened within them. That's why this dad in this mural was speaking at this rally.

By 2021, the political conversation about incarceration had changed. A slate of sentencing reforms started to appear, some born from the practical infeasibility of maintaining such over-crowded prisons. We even ended a key tenet of Proposition 21—the direct filing of youth into adult court—through the youth justice movement's own ballot initiative called Proposition 57.

Malik was now an adult. He had completed every program and educational opportunity he could while inside, just as the political conversation around prisons was changing on the outside.

Shortly thereafter, Salah called De-Bug to say that his son had received a letter from the public defender suggesting that he could be a beneficiary of some of these new reform laws. Salah met with the public defender, who explained that the laws around felony murder had changed and Malik could possibly be released because his current sentence was no longer legal. People with the same charge profiles as Malik were coming home. The attorney filed all the motions to get Malik out, but the Santa Clara DA's office fought for him to stay inside. They challenged the constitution-ality of the law change. They didn't want Malik or anyone who would benefit from the reform to get out. Malik's legal team ap-pealed and won, fortifying the change in the felony murder rule against other DA attacks.

After numerous hearings, which included Salah submitting a social biography video and packet for the attorney to use, Malik was released in the early months of 2022. He had been incarcer-ated since 2007. Seeing Malik walk into De-Bug and sit down at the same table where fourteen years earlier his father first dropped down that folder was surreal. He erased his name from the same board it had been written on for years. That moment was a testament to how an unrelenting devotion to freedom can overcome a fate that the system deemed sealed.

When Malik came to De-Bug for the first time, we took a picture of him and his dad with the mural. They joked about how different Salah looked back then. Now when we give the tour of the space, we have a different, beautiful ending to the story of Salah's mural.

The lesson we learned is that postconviction freedom is won when families and communities refuse to accept the system's declaration as the final word. It's just the next stage of the struggle, regardless of what's in print in those transcripts. To the system, after a sentence is rendered, that bang of the gavel signals the end of the process. But to so many, it's the starting gun of their marathon to freedom. The stories in the following section share the rest of the journey of those trying to get home years, sometimes decades, after an initial sentence was imposed.

New Orleans, Louisiana
Freeing Ourselves to Free Others
Fox Richardson and Rob Richardson
PARTICIPATORY DEFENSE MOVEMENT OF
NEW ORLEANS HUB

We first discovered the model of participatory defense in 2017 at the National Council of Formerly Incarcerated Women and Girls conference, and thought it was the most incredible tool we have found for justice-involved people and their families. They say "to be free is to free others." That is the motto we have lived by since being released from prison in 2018 through clemency. It is the same philosophy that led us to launch Participatory Defense Movement—New Orleans (PDMNola) in 2019, just six months after our family's exodus from Angola State Penitentiary.

Please allow us to introduce ourselves: we are Fox and Rob Richardson, a formerly incarcerated couple who spent *twenty-one years* behind bars before being reunited. We discovered that what took us twenty-one years to learn through trial and error was now built into a model so that other justice-involved families would not have to endure what our family went through. There was now a road map, a support system, a community working alongside you to teach the techniques and strategies required to "protect your people." We knew that participatory defense was work we must endeavor to do, especially considering how many of our loved ones we had left behind—our co-defendant and nephew Ontario in particular, but also countless others that were now seeking our help after our victory in bringing Rob home. We knew that if we could bring this tool back to our home state of Louisiana—the most incarcerated place on the planet—then we could put the power back into the hands of the people closest to the pain. Three years later, that is exactly what we have done.

PDMNola was founded in April 2019 by Lisa Finch, Sibil Fox, and Robert Richardson. Our two campaigns were freeing our nephew who was arrested with us and the longest-serving woman in this country, Gloria Dean Williams, aka #freemamaglo—neither of which would be easy. One would take the passage of legislation and the latter would require the governor's signature. However, having seen firsthand the power of what is possible through our own family's liberation, we knew liberation was possible.

Gloria Williams had served almost fifty years in prison when we launched her campaign in 2019. She had left behind five children when she entered prison in 1971, the year Fox was born. Initially, we thought that gaining the governor's ear for such a matter would not be such a huge undertaking considering the circumstances: her age (seventy-five), the amount of time served (a whopping fifty years), and the mitigating circumstances of the crime: MamaGlo was not immediately responsible for the robbery-turned-death. What we had not calculated was the resistance to forgiveness that the victims harbored, and the administration's disdain for the fact that MamaGlo had run—on more than one occasion. Yet, having seen miracles performed, we determined it was not our responsibility to "know the way"; our work was just to show to the court actors and decision makers why Ms. Williams deserved to be free.

The saying "Enough pressure on any pipe will make it burst" felt relevant to us. The participatory defense movement is that pressure, and when applied properly it has the force to make the pipes of this system burst wide open! The floodgates opened on July 25, 2019, when the Louisiana Board of Pardons granted a recommendation for clemency to Gloria Williams. And after much petitioning and strategizing, on August 18, 2021 (Fox's fiftieth birthday), Louisiana governor John Bel Edwards signed Gloria's petition. On January 25, 2022, MamaGlo was released into the arms of her four surviving children (her baby girl passed in an accident in 2020).

With this victory serving as wind beneath our wings, we continued our mission of bringing home our dearly beloved nephew, Ontario Smith. Rob had been working on geriatric parole since 2013 as a way to come home, but our claims were denied in the courts, leaving Rob to exit prison through clemency. However, the work on the issue remained a priority. We knew, according to the law, folks like our family member, who had been sentenced to a term of thirty years or more but not life and had served twenty years and reached the age of forty-five, were eligible for parole consideration through Louisiana's geriatric parole law—however, there had been an erroneous interpretation of the law leading to the denial of the right to countless men and women.

As we say during our weekly hub meeting to honor Assata Shakur, "It is our duty to fight for our freedom, it is our duty to win." We continued to pursue relief for our nephew to whom this measure applied, as well as others. And on August 1, 2021, those efforts would prevail with the enactment of Act 122, granting the aforementioned citizens behind bars their right to a parole hearing. This has been one of the most significant works we have accomplished, as this measure alone not only granted our nephew an opportunity for parole, it now granted parole consideration to over three thousand incarcerated citizens in Louisiana.

So, you know what happens next! Well . . . when we fight, we win!!!

On February 18, 2022, our nephew Ontario, who had been sentenced to forty-five years alongside Rob's sixty-year sentence, was granted parole and was released from prison on June 6, 2022, having served twenty-five years behind bars. Our efforts returned him home to his parents, three children, and two grandchildren. This is undoubtedly the greatest testament to the power of this work and the families doing it.

Our hub, which is now expanding all over the state of Louisiana and growing from PDMNola to PDMLouisiana, counts our success by how much time we save an individual from spending behind bars as opposed to how much time they have been sentenced to serve. To date, we have saved over 3,300 years of TIME. Yes, we are time-savers! We are giving back the one thing none of us can create—TIME. This is just the beginning. Working alongside this national movement with hubs all across this country, we are building an army of freedom fighters that are not taking things as they are, but making them the way we know they should be.

Oakland, California
Transforming Trauma into Triumph
John Vasquez

OAKLAND PARTICIPATORY DEFENSE HUB

"Once a gang member, always a gang member." I'll never forget these words from the district attorney as I was prosecuted and processed through adult court when I was only sixteen. The criminal legal system is not broken; it is operating just as it was intended. I intentionally refrain from using the phrase "justice" system because how can a system that negatively and disproportionally impacts low-income families of color be just? The system is designed to isolate families and friends from their loved ones as they make their journey through the court system, and it is often a confusing, frustrating, and despairing experience. The courtroom landscape is based on power and control similar to an abusive and exploitative relationship. The system is designed to make people feel powerless, hopeless—passive observers rather than active participants. Participatory defense changes the power dynamics in the courtroom while leveling the playing field so that people facing criminal charges and their families have a fighting chance. That's why I believe in the participatory defense model and the community power it creates in those who feel overwhelmed and defeated by the system. I do this work because my own journey through the system was traumatic and disempowering. I also do this work for my family. Lived experience has shown me that many of the people who suffer most are the families of incarcerated people, when their only crime is caring for their incarcerated loved one.

It's been nearly thirty years, but I still vividly recall how isolated and powerless my family felt when I was processed through the court system. By sharing my story, I don't intend to disregard or ignore the very real traumas and harm done to victims and survivors of crimes. I acknowledge that there must be a level of accountability whenever harm is done to individuals and the community. My hope is that one day there will be a *real* system of accountability where transformative justice rather than retributive "justice" prevails. The current adversarial system in the United States does not create an environment of accountability, but rather perpetuates victimization and harm to all parties involved, including the free community. Another injustice of the criminal legal system is that it deliberately ignores the context in which crime occurs. It systematically dehumanizes the person facing charges in order to justify overly harsh prison sentences and punishment. Moreover, the system intentionally uses inflammatory language such as "superpredator," "gang member," and "criminal" as a strategy to weaponize juries, judges, and the public to go along with these harmful practices. When I went through the court system, my traumatic upbringing was completely ignored and even used against me. That story should have been told because it shows that I wasn't a "bad person" who was incorrigible, just a young person trying to survive tremendous hardships and pains. Every person facing charges has a story, and that story needs to be told if we are to have true justice.

I grew up in a single-parent household where my mother was forced to take on the role as sole provider for me and my younger brother. I later found out that both of my parents suffered from their own unresolved childhood trauma that negatively impacted their life outcomes. At an early age, my parents struggled with drug addiction and never graduated from high school. They divorced when I was four years old, and I was devastated. My father came in and out of my life but he never overcame his addiction, never held down a job, and never provided child support. He also served time in prison. Growing up, we often didn't have food in the house, so my little brother and I bounced around to different family members while my mother struggled with her addiction and to make ends meet.

My father died from cirrhosis when I was fifteen, just as he began spending more time in my life. He was only thirty-four. I didn't know how to cope with his death or how to talk to anyone about how I was feeling, so I ran the streets with my neighborhood peer group. The peer group was there for me at a time when I felt like no one else was and I felt like they understood me. My peer group gave me a sense of belonging, and for the first time in my life, I felt important. At sixteen years old, I was tried as an adult and sentenced to thirty-one years to life for killing a rival gang member. This was during the height of the "superpredator" mania when kids were often deemed incorrigible.

They sent me to a maximum-security prison. One of the guards told me, "Hey youngster, do yourself a favor and hang yourself. You're never getting out of here." And he was right. Back in the nineties, lifers weren't getting out. I had no hope of ever coming home, so I didn't even try to better my life because life was never going to get any better.

In 2001, I was put in solitary confinement. It was the first time in my life I was alone with my thoughts and four walls. I did a lot of soul-searching and came to the realization that my lifestyle was revictimizing my victims and hurting those who loved and cared about me. I wanted to change but didn't know how, so I prayed and asked God for help. Suddenly it felt like a huge weight lifted from my shoulders, and although I was still doing a life sentence, I never felt freer.

Transformation didn't come overnight. I started reading self-help books, attending groups, and began processing all the emotional trauma I bottled in as a child—trauma I suppressed for so long that I didn't even know I had. I got actively involved in my community behind prison walls. I created curriculum for two dozen self-help workshops, co-founded a youth mentoring program, and started another program that quickly grew to over 200 participants and is still going strong today. I earned six associate's degrees with honors and wrote articles for the prison newsletter. Prior to my parole hearing, I put together a packet highlighting my accountability in action, remorse, accomplishments, parole plans, and support system. My mother was my biggest advocate. She tirelessly collected letters of support and located resources for me that would be beneficial once I returned to the free community.

After serving twenty-five years, the parole board found me suitable for release. I was so happy that I cried tears of joy. Adjusting to society was challenging because I literally stepped into the future. I immediately got actively involved in my community and joined the community clean team picking up trash on San Francisco's skid row. I also volunteered at a youth violence prevention program. I worked two part-time jobs making a dollar above minimum wage and put myself through school graduating summa cum laude from San Francisco State University with a BA in Sociology and minor in Criminal Justice Studies. In 2020, I was selected for a fellowship that allowed me to intern in Supervisor Shamann Walton's office representing District 10 in San Francisco and participated in the "Close Juvenile Hall" working group. Today, I am the policy and legal services manager at Communities United for Restorative Youth Justice, an organization that mobilizes young leaders in the movement to end youth criminalization and mass incarceration. I support families in bringing their incarcerated loved ones home through participatory defense, families that are in the situation mine was in all those years go.

My own journey going through the court system and incarceration gives me a unique insider perspective into how the system actually works, which is often different than how it's supposed to work in principle. Moreover, my lived experience of being formerly incarcerated allows me to build trusted relationships with participatory defense participants as a credible messenger. After hearing me share my own story of incarceration, many of the participants that I've had the privilege of supporting have expressed a renewed sense of hope that their loved one will someday come home just like I have, particularly those with loved ones serving or facing life sentences. I do this work because I understand through my own experience that people, no matter what they may have done in their lives, are worthy of opportunities to heal, grow, and thrive. No one is born a criminal. People's decisions are often influenced by their life situations, which means that context should be considered when a person is facing charges, especially when childhood trauma is involved. Prisons and jails not only lack environments for healing and rehabilitation; they actually have the opposite effect by perpetuating environments of trauma.

Fortunately for me, despite these surroundings and after many years of hopelessness and desperation, I was able to begin my healing journey and transform my trauma into triumph. I couldn't have done this without the support of God, family, friends, and community.

Due to years of movement work up and down the state, California now has different pathways for people who have been dramatically oversentenced to possibly come home. Unfortunately, many of these reform laws don't automatically release people back to their families and communities; the person has to make the case for freedom. Oftentimes, the key to that victory is sharing what loved ones have achieved in prison, demonstrating their positive changes, and highlighting the strong support system that awaits them at home. Having traveled this long and arduous journey myself, I've been able to use my lived experience as a guide for families on how to create and articulate a personal narrative that highlights insight, accountability, and remorse, all of which increase a person's chances of obtaining freedom after being excessively sentenced by overzealous district attorneys.

My lived experience also has been a tool in making the case for release through our hub. Drawing from my time inside, my past, what I went through and witnessed, I have also been tapped into by defense attorneys as a "subject matter expert" in prison conditions and gangs, and have lent my expertise in several court cases.

One such case was Miguel, who had already served twenty-six years for a crime that was committed when he was only eighteen. Miguel had already won his petition for resentencing under California's SB 1437 felony murder law, which gives people an opportunity to have their murder charge dismissed if they were not the person who committed the actual killing. However, the judge had the discretion to sentence Miguel to time served or to serve another decade in prison. The DA was hell-bent on keeping Miguel in prison and was using Miguel's past gang involvement as justification for not letting him return to his family. After his family planned with the attorney, I was called in to do an assessment regarding these concerns. I reviewed Miguel's social history investigation report, disciplinary reports, psychological evaluation, character letters, rehabilitative and educational achievements, relapse prevention plan, and parole plan. I also interviewed Miguel at length.

Having lived a gang lifestyle myself (inside and outside of prison), then having turned my life around and facilitated several dismantling gang associations workshops, I am very familiar with what behavior patterns and beliefs to look for in determining whether someone is on their healing journey out of the gang lifestyle or still stuck in their traumas. Based upon the evidence presented before me, it was clear that Miguel had made significant lifestyle changes, was well on his way to the path of personal transformation, and would be an asset to the free community if released. I submitted an in-depth report to the presiding judge and showed up to testify in court. Fortunately, the judge was able to see Miguel's positive transformation and he made a determination to give him time served. The DA was furious, but Miguel's family was elated to have him back home.

It is so important to have community experts with lived experience and knowledge to counter law enforcement's gang "experts" who do not have the relevant lived experience and who oftentimes use the "gang" label to dehumanize people and weaponize juries and judges to convict people and oversentence them. This cycle of abuse, dehumanization, and excessive sentencing leads to people fighting for their freedom years and decades later through the parole process or resentencing opportunities. It is a very challenging task for incarcerated people and their families, which makes participatory defense support so important because it often means the difference between more years, sometimes entire decades, of traumatizing incarceration or freedom and family reunification. Personal experience has shown me that so-called "gang members" and "violent offenders" (labels given to me) can be positive assets to their families and communities if only given the chance to come home.

Nashville, Tennessee
To Fight Is to Win
Dawn Harrington
FREE HEARTS HUB

When I was at Rikers, I used to sit at this table with a couple of people in the day room every day. We would hang out, get to know each other. People treated us as outcasts for a bit. One officer even called us the "MO" crew. I learned later that it meant "mental observation" because I guess a lot of the people I sat with lived with mental health issues. It didn't matter. We became really good friends.

One of the people that I always sat with was getting ready to get out. We were all excited for her. It was a Friday, and we all celebrated with her. We were so happy. That Monday, I was working at the jail clinic, where people getting booked into the jail had to stop in during intake. And that's when I saw her. Our friend. And she looked like a train wreck. So much so that she didn't even recognize who I was.

That moment really shook me. I didn't know at the time the kind of impact it would make, but I really just started grappling with all of the different issues that arise with incarceration. I journaled about it, and that's when the idea of Free Hearts came into being. It was inside the jail cell, on my bed, that I wanted to create a way to make sense of my experiences while incarcerated.

I left Rikers after a year and went back to Tennessee to bring what I wrote in my journal to life. That's when Free Hearts was founded as an organization led by formerly incarcerated women providing support, education, and advocacy and organizing to families impacted by incarceration, with the ultimate goals of reuniting families and strengthening communities. When we first started, we wanted to offer so many things because our experiences showed us that the system needed to be dramatically transformed, and we had such a huge need for our community. However, one of our founding members strongly encouraged us to start small based on our capacity, so we started by doing support groups only within the Nashville women's jail. We wanted to build relationships and trust and figure out what the needs were of the women inside. We wanted to build out our organization slowly and surely, grounded in the actual needs that families impacted by incarceration had.

We started in the Nashville jail, bringing in blank needs-assessment forms that basically just had a place for their name and prisoner number. We left an open space where they could write what their needs were. We learned quickly not to do it that way because people wrote everything from "Go to my car that's in impound and try to get my stuff back," to "Contact my Mama and tell her to bring my child for a visit," to "Try reach out to Metro Development Housing Association (MDHA) to try to buy time so I don't lose my housing," to "Try to get me approval to get into treatment"; and the list went on and on.

On one of the days in our support group, we had all of the women make name placards. A young, pretty, petite Black woman named Shantonio, with small plaits in her hair and glasses and a quiet, sweet, and creative demeanor, made hers so colorful and beautiful. It had the gentlest handwriting to the point that it looked like calligraphy. She was so helpful and even a little timid in our first meeting. So it was a shock after we got back to the office and reviewed the forms from that day to learn that Shantonio put on her needs assessment that she needed help with her case because she was facing life due to her abuser killing her three-year-old son, Elijah.

That was the moment in time that families from San Jose's leading participatory defense found us, and we found them. Shantonio's became one of the first families we rallied around to support. We read through police reports, helped gather and prep witnesses, and made a social biography packet to tell the larger story of Shantonio. At the time, the district attorney was touting his commitment to restorative justice, and we even went to conferences to meet with him to present Shantonio's case and to offer restorative justice as an option. We also pointed out the disparities in charging among Black and white women in similar cases like this. He'd promise to meet with us, then would fade to black.

Shantonio was willing to take a plea and was facing trial. But she didn't think she could bear reliving those unspeakable moments in her life. Her body wouldn't let her—she would get some of the worst anxiety we had seen. To prepare for court days, we would try to help her cope, breathe, workshop in every way possible. But on the day of court, the DA offered to go two years down from the original offer of thirty years.

Twenty-eight years. And that's the plea she took.

I remember a point in my life when I took the plea that led me to Rikers. Everyone around me was telling me it was over—everything was over for me. They were crying for me. They were, like, there's nothing you can do. Just accept it. It wasn't until I saw a friend of mine, P Moses, who told me it wasn't. She was the only one who told me that. She said, "Don't let them dance up on you like that, railroad you." I don't even know if she knew what that meant then or what "It's not over" looked like, but it did light a fire in me.

I shared those words with Shantonio and her family at the moment she took the plea. It wasn't going to be over until she came home. Even on the days leading up to trial, we told her, Look, no matter what happens here, it's not the final say. It's never over until you're home, and no matter what happens, we are going to be still with you. Being able to share that with Shantonio—who I knew was sitting in the same universe of feelings—I felt I could give her those words with a whole set of tools, strategies, and the backing of participatory defense. It didn't mean we couldn't lick our wounds after this loss, but we pick ourselves back up and keep going.

With Shantonio, as with our loved ones that we organize with long-term, we thought about what's the next step. We don't think "Nothing can be done." We're always thinking about the next thing that *can* be done. We always encourage people to believe that it's never the final say until they hit their freedom dream. We looked at different avenues of postconviction relief, and that's really what got us as a hub to support a lot more families who were in that stage, who felt stuck, who felt maybe the light was dim but were going to hold on to it. We worked with Shantonio's first and second attorneys in her appeal process. One didn't do much; the other felt like he did a little more but was not very responsive. We kept highlighting all the issues we saw during the case and really presenting who Shantonio was to them through the social biography to see how to challenge the plea. As more and more families came to the hub whose loved ones were inside the prison, we grew in our knowledge of different steps to take in postconviction relief and how to get loved ones back to court to get their sentences reviewed or cases relooked at. Sometimes it's working with the families to get their loved ones' court and prison files, contacting their former attorneys or appellate attorneys just to even see what avenues their loved ones have tried, what we want to try, and what we want to create.

For a lot of the women in our jail program, we often had seen that a lot of them wanted their family members to be involved in participatory defense. They would give us a long list of people, and we would get them involved and it would be a tangible way for them to get involved and support their loved ones. Women often get fewer people visiting them in the prisons. The ones who hold up the women are often other women in the family who are also taking care of their children. But with participatory defense, families can be involved in their own ways because we think of real steps they can take to become active in the cases. We do participatory defense inside the jails and with the families.

It was always a goal of ours to develop new leadership and it is also key to the model of participatory defense. Families must get involved in and lead the process. We were able to stipend one of first members so she could help out with the roles of the hub. Others of our members train and develop the leadership of other members. Some members bring in new members, getting the word out, and so forth and so on. It's because of them that we know our hub, and ultimately our state will have a bright future.

When traditional appeal processes were exhausted, we explored clemency—and looking at the power of governors to grant release or some kind of reprieve. We thought there had to be someone outside of the court system whom we could approach. We saw that the governor was only granting one a year or so, and we wanted to expand that—to tap into his power to grant mass releases through clemency. We had been working with the National Council for Incarcerated and Formerly Incarcerated Women and Girls to explore this larger campaign.

While the COVID pandemic shut the world down, it also exposed the most vulnerable. Because the courts were all shut down, we laid our sights on the governor to use his power to free people. At that time, the governor ran on criminal justice reform, so we wanted to push him on it. We had a list of 122 people for whom clemency was their best option during that time. We partnered with our movement family at Community Defense of East Tennessee and Concerned Citizens for Justice, and others like No Exceptions Prison Collective, to really organize for power statewide. We helped organize car rallies and protests at the governor's house to really highlight his power to grant clemency.

In 2022, one of the first loved ones we put forward for clemency—Mindy—came home. She was one of five people who had powerful stories expressed through social bio packets and a very public social media campaign. While the Tennessee parole board voted for a recommendation for her sentence to be commuted, we pushed the governor to commute her sentence to time served. She came home in 2022, and as we uplifted her story as a survivor, we also highlighted that Black women, especially those who are criminalized survivors of violence, should be given the same chance.

Throughout all the families' experiences, we have seen patterns of repression that exist across cases. Police target Black families in our neighborhoods, even killing loved ones. I live in the zip code 37208, which carries one of the highest incarceration rates in the country of people my age, my skin color. My hope borders on optimism. Sometimes I forget that I live in a state where white supremacy, misogyny, and patriarchy are so deeply entrenched. But with Mindy's situation, it gave me hope for Shantonio—that whoever needs to see this, who has the power to act, can see the inequalities of the system and grant her a chance at coming home too. We're happy for Mindy, but we have to continue to keep putting our loved ones' stories through social bios front and center to get community support so the governor knows he's making the right decision.

Shantonio is one of the loved ones we hope to bring home—through postconviction relief either through clemency, a re-review of her case, or law change. Through the years since 2017, we've reunited families, saved over 967 years of time—meaning families together, made whole. We know we just have to keep going. We have to create more innovations, more ways to expand clemency and postconviction options, so that loved ones like Shantonio can heal.

That's why we don't stop at just sentencing. Participatory defense, at its heart, is about family. And our hope reflects that. We have witnessed strong acts of resistance. Our first organizer, Mama Gloria, had successfully negotiated on a plea deal for one of her sons, getting it down ten years from the supposed "best deal" the district attorney had to offer. We know that it's possible in all stages of the process, as long as we keep our eyes on the prize: our loved ones home. Like Brother Kenneth, who's one of our hub members, reminds us, "You already won the fight because you're in the fight!"

A new world is possible. And in some ways, it is already here!

EPILOGUE

CASES TO CAMPAIGNS

S ometimes the discipline of participatory defense requires the work to happen beyond the courts—to challenge the systems and rules that are the very foundation of that institution. When people are working on freeing loved ones, or protecting them from incarceration, that battle requires them to look under the hood of the criminal punishment system, to see how the carceral engine works. While that has tactical value for an individual case, it also exposes where collective power can be applied to challenge the machine itself. Families who attended the participatory defense meetings in San Jose all those years ago, even before there was a national network, are examples of this natural growth from singular individual case advocacy to system-challenging organizing.

After Blanca saved her son Rudy from a wrongful charge based on a false confession, she joined other parents, public defenders, and youth justice organizers to advocate for the first ever Miranda Rights for Youth law, which mandated that youth under the age of sixteen speak with a defense attorney before police are allowed to interrogate them. Blanca and other parents contributed to getting the law passed through a social media campaign that shared the number of hours they were separated from their children during interrogation, the impact of that coercive process on the case, and the lasting impact on their children, even after the case was over.

Similarly, as Gail was fighting to stop sixteen-year-old Joe from being charged as an adult, she also joined the fight to help pass a law, Proposition 57, that prevented any youth in California from being directly filed into the adult system by a prosecutor. To protect Joe was also to protect countless other youth Gail would never meet.

In every participatory defense meeting, without it being named, there exists a circulatory, replenishing, dynamic potential of personal struggle and collective campaign. This same movement physics of "cases to campaigns" has occurred at hubs across the country. In Pennsylvania, the hubs are working to end juvenile incarceration entirely. In Tennessee, the Knoxville hub turned a social biography video into an outward facing documentary to successfully organize for the ending of juvenile life without parole. In Louisiana, the hubs have taken their postconviction work from the local court to the steps of the capitol to advocate with others for mass clemency.

Viewed through this lens, participatory defense is as much of a movement-leader locator device as it is a tool to challenge an individual incarceration. It reveals the latent and powerful leadership capacity of everyday people.

The campaigns and initiatives participatory defense hubs initiate and lead look as unique and different as each person who comes to a weekly meeting and the circumstances that brought them. But as the stories in this book show, these people share a unifying vision of reunification and freedom.

To me, the work of participatory defense practitioners is an expression of something older, and more inevitable, than the story of incarceration in the United States itself. It is kindred to what Buddha described on the road to liberation as a "sangha." Thousands of years ago, in an ancient language called Pali, the Buddha explained his meditative practice by saying that one needed eyes to see the path, and legs to walk it. As organizers today, we interpret this as "theory" and "practice." But the Buddha also spoke of a third foundation to the path—a sangha—which is a community of practitioners all seeking their own liberation. Those participatory defense meetings are a sangha—a community coming together with all seeking their own liberation while supporting the journey of others. And in that way, it shows that liberation need not be a solitary or lonely walk. It is found through community.

PUBLISHING IN THE
PUBLIC INTEREST

Thank you for reading this book published by The New Press. The New Press is a nonprofit, public interest publisher. New Press books and authors play a crucial role in sparking conversations about the key political and social issues of our day.

We hope you enjoyed this book and that you will stay in touch with The New Press. Here are a few ways to stay up to date with our books, events, and the issues we cover:

- Sign up at www.thenewpress.com/subscribe to receive updates on New Press authors and issues and to be notified about local events
- Like us on Facebook: www.facebook.com/newpressbooks
- Follow us on Twitter: www.twitter.com/thenewpress
- Follow us on Instagram: www.instagram.com/thenew press

Please consider buying New Press books for yourself; for friends and family; or to donate to schools, libraries, community centers, prison libraries, and other organizations involved with the issues our authors write about.

The New Press is a 501(c)(3) nonprofit organization. You can also support our work with a tax-deductible gift by visiting www .thenewpress.com/donate.